The Black Grimoire

Lucifer LeGivorden

For my love, Diana

Also by Lucifer LeGivorden:

The Satanic Testament

The Satanic Testament:
Expanded & Revised Edition

Gothos Saga Book 1: Dark Awakening

Table of contents

Introduction

Before we begin, it should be noted that this book is by no means complete. Or at least in my opinion that is. It is my hope that as the years progress this book will see new editions and expansions, with many rituals added.

It has taken me many years of compiling and testing out rituals to finally put together a comprehensive list of viable, usable rituals, that would leave even the stingiest and uptight Church of Satan members feeling satisfied.

I first got the notion to create this book years ago when during rituals I found myself very frustrated with the difficulty I had, literally bouncing between published books with tiny fonts, to put together a single cohesive ritual. A very difficult and infuriating feet in an endarkend Ritual Chamber.

I felt that surely a better way could be done to simplify the whole procedure, and make it easier on the reader.

As the years have gone on, I have managed to put together a series of rituals. Cleaned up and compiled together in an easy to read format for myself. Literally treating them as though they were to be read by the elderly and near sighted. The irony being that I now find myself reading as an older man with glasses perched precariously on top of my head.

The document that follows is that selfsame compiled list of rituals that I keep on official record for my own small organization with only one having never been used at the time of publishing this document.

It should be noted that each of these rituals is a Black Mass in and of itself. Though there are three official Black Masses contained within. Each service is as detailed as one can be, sparing nothing, and fully enabling the reader to effectively perform the rituals without trouble, or jumping from one book or section to another.

It is my hope that you find these rituals as fun and exciting as I and my members have. I also hope you find this to be a handy and welcome tome into your occult library.

So, it is now that without further adue, I present here in the same vein as LaVeys Satanic Rituals,

The Black Grimiore.

The Satanic High Mass

The core ritual in modern Satanism, especially any sort of Laveyan Satanism, is the High Mass. This ritual contains all of the prime elements found in Satanic Ritual, and is thus the prime example of the modern Satanic Ritual. But it was not always so, and has taken several decades to become the full ritual presented here.

When Anton LaVey first began his religion, he was often prone to "Winging it" so to speak. We can see this in various documentaries depicting him in ritual. This was vital for Satanism because it hammered out the fine details. By the time LaVeys bible was published, the core ritual procedurals had begun to take a functional shape.

The cookie cutter format presented for the Satanic ritual would become a staple point for many of the rituals used for many years. It provided a basic outline that was easy to follow for most, only swapping out one or two minor sections depending on the ritual being done.

This would become the mainstay for many years. But in 2006 a new variation was presented to the public. The first fully public viewing of a full High Mass. This would combine the three prime rituals into one event and would be the first full formation of a true core ceremony.

The High Mass presented here is the result of several years of study and research, compiled from several different sources to recreate with some minor modification for personal touch, the High Mass performed by the Church of Satan on 6-6-06.

Generally speaking, the High Mass should be performed twice a month, on full and new moons. This is done to present a stable cycle of the rituals and give the practitioners a foundation to work from.

Music suitable for this rite, is Lustmord's Rising album, which was used during the 6-6-06 event. All the normal ritual supplies for ritual are used here.

The High Mass

I. PURIFICATION OF THE AIR
Ring bell 9 times, directing tolling to the four cardinal compass points while turning counter-clockwise. The "Hymn to Satan" or other appropriate music is played simultaneously.

II. INVOCATION TO SATAN
Celebrant faces the Sigil of the Baphomet with arms spread gently with palms open. Invocation is intoned by Celebrant.

In nomine Dei nostri Satanas Luciferi excelsi!

In the name of Satan, the Ruler of the earth, the King of the world, I command the forces of Darkness to bestow their Infernal power upon me!
Open wide the gates of Hell and come forth from the abyss to greet me as your brother (sister) and friend!
Grant me the indulgences of which I speak! I have taken thy name as a part of myself! I live as the beasts of the field, rejoicing in the fleshly life! I favor the just and curse the rotten! By all the Gods of the Pit, I command that these things of which I speak shall come to pass!
Come forth and answer to your names by manifesting my desires!

OH HEAR THE NAMES!

Congregation repeats each name after Celebrant.

THE INFERNAL NAMES

Abaddon	Nyarlathotep	Mictian
Euronymous	Baalberith	Tchort
O-ama	Mammon	Cimeries
Adramelech	Sedit	Cthulhu
Fenriz	Balaam	Anton LaVey
Pan	Mania	Coyote
Ahpuch	Sekhmet	Milcom
Gorgo	Baphomet	Thamuz
Pluto	Mantus	Dagon
Ahriman	Set	Moloch
Haborym	Bast	Thoth
Proserpine	Marduk	Damballa
Amon	Shaitan	Mormo
Hecate	Beelzebub	Tunrida
Pwcca	Mastema	Demogorgon
Apollyn	Shamad	Naamah
Ishtar	Behemoth	Typhon
Rimmon	Melek Taus	Diabolus
Asmodeus	Shiva	Nergal
Kali	Beherit	Yaotzin
Sabazios	Mephistopheles	Vlad Dracula
Astaroth	Yog-Sothoth	Nihasa
Lilith	Supay	Yen-lo-Wang
Sammael	Bilé	Emma-O
Azazel	Metztli	Nija
Loki	T'an-mo	O-Yama
Samnu	Chemosh	Shub-Nigguath

Celebrant: "Arise oh Gods of the Abyss and manifest thy presence through thy blessing."

III. RITE OF THE CHALICE
Celebrant adds incense to the burner.

Celebrant: "As our incense ascends to thee, Infernal Lord, so shall your blessings descend upon us."
Cense chalice three times, bow. Cense baphomet again three times, and bow.
Perform a circuit around the chamber counterclockwise and direct
Incense to the cardinal points.

Bless chalice with the mudras of flames.

Celebrant: "Lord Satan, Imperator of Fire, Hell and Earth are filled with your glory.
Hosanna in profundis!"

Celebrant elevates chalice.

Gong is struck.

Celebrant: "Behold the chalice of ecstasy filled with the elixir of life. As kindred to the undefiled beasts, I drink and celebrate the Black Flame within."

Celebrant drinks and says: "Satan, thy strength is mine!"

Celebrant turns to offer chalice to mourners with these words:

Celebrant: "Drink and honor thy true nature."

Participants who wish to partake approach. They each drink and reply:

Participant: "The Black Flame burns within me. Satan, thy strength is mine!"

Celebrant faces altar and elevates chalice a final time.

Celebrant: "Hail Satan!"

Congregation. (responds): "Hail Satan!"

Gong is struck.

Celebrant replaces the chalice on altar.

IV. SUMMONING THE PRINCES OF HELL
Celebrant takes sword or Athame and points towards the domain of the Prince to be called.

Celebrant: "From the south I summon thee almighty Satan. Come forth oh Lord of the Inferno, I bid thee welcome!"

"From the east I summon thee great Lucifer. Come forth oh Bearer of Light, I bid thee welcome!"

"From the north I summon thee fearsome Belial. Come forth oh King of the Earth, I bid thee welcome!"

"From the west I summon thee dread Leviathan. Come forth oh Dragon of the Abyss, I bid thee welcome!"

"Shemhamforash!"

Congregation. (responds): "Shemhamforash!"

Gong is struck.

Celebrant: "Hail Satan!"

Congregation. (responds): "Hail Satan!"

Gong is struck.

Celebrant replaces sword on altar.

V. BENEDICTION
Celebrant elevates phallus:

Celebrant: "For though art a mighty Lord, oh Satan, and from thee arises all potency, justice, and dominion. Let our visions become reality and our creations endure, for we are your kindred, demon brethren, scions of carnal joy."

Celebrant shakes phallus towards appropriate compass points saying:

"Satan, give to us thy blessing."

"Lucifer, grant to us thy favor."

"Belial, confer upon us thy benisons."

"Leviathan, bestow to us thy treasures."

Celebrant replaces phallus on the altar.

VI. THE READING

Celebrant: "A reading from the Book of Satan!"
Congregation. (responds): "Glory to thee, Prince of Darkness!"

1. Life is the great indulgence - death, the great abstinence. Therefore, make the most of life - HERE AND NOW!

2. There is no heaven of glory bright, and no hell where sinners roast. Here and now is our day of torment! Here and now is our day of joy! Here and now is our opportunity! Choose ye this day, this hour, for no redeemer liveth!

3. Say unto thine own heart, "I am mine own redeemer."

4. Stop the way of them that would persecute you. Let those who devise thine undoing be hurled back to confusion and infamy. Let them be as chaff before the cyclone and after they have fallen rejoice in thine own salvation.

5. Then all thy bones shall say pridefully, "Who is like unto me? Have I not been too strong for mine adversaries? Have I not delivered MYSELF by mine own brain and body?"

VII. The Canon

Celebrant: (congragants repeat) Our Father which art in Hell, un hallowed is Thy name. Thy kingdom is come, Thy will is done; on earth as it is in Hell! We take this night our rightful due, and trespass not on paths of pain. Lead us unto temptation, and deliver us from false piety, for Thine is the kingdom and the power and the glory forever!

"Shemhamforash!"

Gong is struck.

VIII. THE INVOCATIONS TO LUST, COMPASION, AND DESTRUCTION

COMPASION

Eighteenth key

(Enochian)
Ilasa micalazoda olapireta ialpereji beliore: das odo
Busadire Oiad ouoaresa caosago:
casaremeji Laiada eranu berinutasa cafafame das ivemeda
aqoso adoho Moz, od maoffasa. Bolape como belioreta
pamebeta. Zodacare od Zodameranu! Odo cicale Qaa.
Zodoreje, lape zodiredo Noco Mada, hoathahe Saitan!

(English)
O thou mighty light and burning flame of comfort!, that
unveilest the glory of Satan to the center of the Earth; in
whom the great secrets of truth have their abiding; that is
called in thy kingdom: "strength through joy", and is not to
be measured. Be thou a window of comfort unto me. Move
therefore, and appear! Open the mysteries of your creation!
Be friendly unto me, for I am the same!, the true
worshipper of the highest and ineffable King of Hell!

Celebrant: W ITH the anger of anguish and the wrath of the
stifled, I pour forth my voices, wrapped in rolling thunder
that you may hear!
Oh great lurkers in the darkness, oh guardians of the way,
oh minions of the might of Thoth! Move and appear!

Present yourselves to us in your benign power, in behalf of one who believes and is stricken with torment.

Isolate him/her in the bulwark of your protection, for he/she is undeserving of anguish and desires it not.

Let that which bears against him/her be rendered powerless and devoid of substance.

Succor him/her through fire and water, earth and air, to regain what he/she has lost.

Strengthen with fire the marrow of our friend and companion, our comrade of the Left-and Path.

Through the power of Satan let the earth and its pleasures re-nter his/her being.

Allow his/her vital salts to flow unhampered, that he/she may savor the carnal nectars of his/her future desires.

Strike dumb his/her adversary, formed or formless, that he/she may emerge joyful and strong from that which afflicts him her.

Allow no misfortune to allay his/her path, for he she is of us, and therefore to be cherished.

Restore him/her to power, to joy, to unending dominion over the reverses that have beset him/her.

Build around and within him /her, the exultant radiance that will herald his/her emergence from the stagnant morass which engulfs him/her.

This we command, in the name of Satan, whose mercies flourish and whose sustenance will prevail!

As Satan reigns so shall his/her own whose name is as this sound: (name) is the vessel whose flesh is as the earth; life everlasting, world without end! Shemhamforash! Hail Satan!

Gong is struck following congregants' response to "Shemhamforash!" and "Hail Satan!"

LUST

Second Enochian

(Enochian)
Adagita vau-pa-ahe zodonugonu fa-a-ipe salada! Vi-i-vau
el! Sobame ial-pereji i-zodazodazod pi-adapehe casarema
aberameji ta ta-labo paracaleda qo-ta lores-el-qo turebesa
ooge balatohe! Giui cahisa lusada oreri od micalapape
cahisa bia ozodonugonu! Iape noanu tarofe coresa tage o-
quo maninu IA-I-DON. Torezodu! gohe-el, zodacare eca
ca-no-quoda! zodameranu micalazodo od ozadazodame
vaurelar; Iape zodir IOIAD!

(English)
Can the wings of the winds hear your voices of wonder? O
you! the great spawn of the worms of the Earth!, whom the
Hell fire frames in the depth of my jaws! Whom I have
prepared as cups for a wedding or as flowers regaling the
chambers of lust! Stronger are your feet than the barren
stone! Mightier are your voices than the manifold winds!
For you are become as a building such as is not, save in the
mind of the All-Powerful manifestation of Satan! "Arise!"
saith the First! Move therefore unto his servants! Show
yourselves in power, and make me a strong seer-of-things,
for I am of Him that liveth forever!

Celebrant: COME forth, Oh great spawn of the abyss and
make thy presence manifest. I have set my thoughts upon
the blazing pinnacle which glows with the chosen lust of
the moments of increase and grows fervent in the turgid
swell.

Send forth that messenger of voluptuous delights, and let these obscene vistas of my dark desires take form in future deeds and doings.

From the sixth tower of Satan there shall come a sign which joineth with those salts within, and as such will move the body of the flesh of my summoning.

I have gathered forth my symbols and prepare my garnishings of theat wich is to be, and the image of my creation lurketh as a seething basilisk awaiting his release. The vision shall become as reality and through the nourishment that my sacrifice giveth, the angles of the first dimension shall become the substance of the third.

Go out into the void of night (light of day) and pierce that mind that respondeth with thoughts which leadeth to paths of lewd abandon.

(Male) My rod is athrust! The penetrating force of my venom shall shatter the sanctity of that mind which is barren of lust; and as the seed falleth, so shall its vapours be spread within that reeling brain benumbing it to helplessness according to my will! In the name of the great god Pan, may my secret thoughts be marshaled into the movements of the flesh of that which I desire! Shemhamforash! Hail Satan!

(Female) My loins are aflame! The dripping of the nectar from my eager cleft shall act as pollen to that slumbering brain, and the mind that feels not lust shall on a sudden reel with crazed impulse. And when my mighty surge is spent, new wanderings shall begin; and that flesh which I desire shall come to me. In the names of the great harlot of Babylon, and of Lilith, and of Hecate, may my lust be fulfilled! Shemhamforash! Hail Satan!

Gong is struck following congregants' response to "Shemhamforash!" and "Hail Satan!"

DESTRUCTION

Seventeenth Key

(Enochian)
Ilasa dial pereta! soba vaupaahe cahisa nanuba zodixalayo
dodasihe od berinuta faxisa hubaro tasataxa yolasa: soba
Iad i Vonupehe o Uonupehe: aladonu dax ila od toatare!
Zodacare od Zodameranu! Odo cicale Qaa! Zodoreje, lape
zodiredo Noco Mada, hoathahe Saitan!

(English)
O thou third flame!, whose wings are thorns to stir up
vexation, and who hast myriad living lamps going before
thee; whose God is wrath in anger - Gird up thy loins and
harken! Move therefore, and appear! Open the mysteries of
your creation! Be friendly unto me, for I am the same!, the
true worshipper of the highest and ineffable King of Hell!

Celebrant: BEHOLD! The mighty voices of my vengeance
smash the stillness of the air and stand as monoliths of
wrath upon a plain of writhing serpents. I am become as a
monstrous machine of annihilation to the festering
fragments of the body of he/she who would detain me.
It repenteth me not that my summons doth ride upon the
blasting winds which multiply the sting of my bitterness;
And great black slimy shapes shall rise from brackish pits
and vomit forth their pustulence into his/her puny brain.

13

I call upon the messengers of doom to slash with grim delight this victim I hath chosen. Silent is that voiceless bird that feeds upon the brain-ulp of him (her) who hath tormented me, and the agony of the is to be shall sustain itself in shrieks of pain, only to serve as signals of warning to those who would resent my being.

Oh come forth in the name of Abaddon and destroy him/her whose name I giveth as a sign.

Oh great brothers of the night, thou who makest my place of comfort, who rideth out upon the hot winds of Hell, who dwelleth in the devil's fane; Move and appear! Present yourselves to him (her) who sustaineth the rottenness of the mind that moves the gibbering mouth that mocks the just and strong!; rend that gaggling tongue and close his/her throat, Oh Kali! Pierce his/her lungs with the stings of scorpions, Oh Sekhmet! Plunge his/her substance into the dismal void, Oh mighty Dagon!

I thrust aloft the bifid barb of Hell and on its tines resplendently impaled my sacrifice through vengeance rests! Shemhamforash! Hail Satan!

Gong is struck following congregants' response to "Shemhamforash!" and "Hail Satan!"

IX. AVE SATANAS
Celebrant: "To us, thy devoted disciples, oh Infernal Lord, who celebrate our iniquity and trust in your boundless might, grant thy bond of Stygian sodality. It is through you that lavish gifts come to us; knowledge, vigor, and wealth are yours to bestow.

We renounce the spiritual paradise of The desperate and gullible. You have won our trust, oh God of the Flesh, for you champion the satisfaction of all our desires and provide abundant fulfillment in the land of the living. Shemhamforash!"

Congreg. (responds): "Shemhamforash!"

Celebrant: "Deliver us, Dark Lord, from every hindrance and grant us joy in our lives. By your munificence you ensue our freedom and protect us from injustice as we indulge in our heart's desires. The kingdom, the power, and the glory are eternally yours."

Celebrant (CONGREG. Repeats): "Hail Satan full of might! Our allegiance is with thee!

Cursed are they, the God adorers, and cursed are the worshippers of the Nazarene Eunuch!

Unholy Satan, bringer of enlightenment, lend us thy power, Now and throughout the hours of our lives!

Shemhamforash!"

X. THE CLOSING RITE

Celebrant: "I bid thee rise and give the Sign of the Horns. (If standing, 'I bid thee give the Sign of the Horns.')" Congregation responds as bidden with the salute, given with the left hand.

Celebrant: "Almighty Satan, open wide the Gates of Hell! Reveal the mysteries of your creation for we are partakers of your undefiled wisdom! Forget ye not what was and is to be! Flesh without sin! World without end!"

Celebrant: (Congregation. repeats): "Shemhamforash!"
"Hail Satan!"
"Hail Satan!"
"Hail Satan!"

Gong is struck following congregants' response to "Shemhamforash!" and each "Hail Satan!"

X. POLLUTIONARY
Celebrant rings bell as at the beginning, while "Hymn to Satan" or music that is appropriate is played. When the sounds have decayed into silence the Celebrant concludes:

Celebrant: "So it is done!"

Celebrant extinguishes remaining illuminating candles or other light sources if this is out of doors, and all experience the darkness for a moment. Conventional illumination is then restored, ending the ceremony.

XII. Celebration
If desired a celebratory feast or after party may take place for the Congregation to relax and unwind.

The Evolved High Mass

This Ritual is a variation of the "Standard High Mass" used by The Satanic Thulian Society members in its early years.

After our formal formation of STS as an organization in which we announced the decision to proceed as if the 1975 Schism between LaVey and Aquino never transpired, it became logical to begin adopting a new hybrid approach to rituals. Incorporating works from the Temple of Set, and other various sources, and adapting them to Satanism proper when necessary. This ritual also perfects a few alternative methods previously touched upon in older versions of the ritual.

It should be noted that this does not replace the Standard High Mass. In truth they are almost identical. However, this gives an alternative version of several parts to STS Priesthood for the sake of diversity in ritual and adaptability for circumstance.

I. PURIFICATION OF THE AIR

Ring bell 9 times, directing tolling to the four cardinal compass points while turning counter-clockwise. The "Hymn to Satan" or other appropriate music is played simultaneously.

II. INVOCATION TO SATAN

Celebrant faces the Sigil of the Baphomet with arms spread gently with palms open. Invocation is intoned by Celebrant.

In nomine Dei nostri Satanas Luciferi excelsi!

In the name of Satan, the Ruler of the earth, the King of the world, I/we invoke the forces of Darkness to bestow their Infernal power upon me/us!

From your throne in Pandemonium, to the Medusa Gate of Dis, and onward to the Vestibule! Open wide the Gates of Hell and come forth from the abyss to greet me/us as your brothers/sisters and friends!

Grant me/us the indulgences of which I/we speak! I/We have taken thy name as a part of myself! I/we live as the beasts of the field, rejoicing in the fleshly life! I/We favor the just and curse the rotten! By all the Gods of the Pit, I/we ask that these things of which I/we speak shall come to pass!

Come forth and answer to your names by manifesting my/our desires!

OH HEAR THE NAMES!

Congregation repeats each name after Celebrant.

THE INFERNAL NAMES

Abaddon	Baalberith	Cimeries
Euronymous	Mammon	Cthulhu
O-ama	Sedit	Anton LaVey
Adramelech	Balaam	Coyote
Fenriz	Mania	Milcom
Pan	Sekhmet	Thamuz
Ahpuch	Baphomet	Dagon
Gorgo	Mantus	Moloch
Pluto	Set	Thoth
Ahriman	Bast	Damballa
Haborym	Marduk	Mormo
Proserpine	Shaitan	Tunrida
Amon	Beelzebub	Demogorgon
Hecate	Mastema	Naamah
Pwcca	Shamad	Typhon
Apollyn	Behemoth	Diabolus
Ishtar	Melek Taus	Nergal
Rimmon	Shiva	Yaotzin
Asmodeus	Beherit	Vlad Dracula
Kali	Mephistopheles	Nihasa
Sabazios	Yog-Sothoth	Yen-lo-Wang
Astaroth	Supay	Emma-O
Lilith	Bilé	Nija
Sammael	Metztli	O-Yama
Azazel	T'an-mo	Shub-Nigguath
Loki	Chemosh	
Samnu	Mictian	
Nyarlathotep	Tchort	

Celebrant: "Arise oh Gods of the Abyss and manifest thy presence through thy blessing."

19

III. RITE OF THE CHALICE
Celebrant adds incense to the burner.

Celebrant: "As our incense ascends to thee, Infernal Lord, so shall your blessings descend upon us."
Cense chalice three times, bow. Cense baphomet again three times, and bow.
Perform a circuit around the chamber counterclockwise and direct
Incense to the cardinal points.

Bless chalice with the mudras of flames.

Celebrant: "Lord Satan, Imperator of Fire, Hell and Earth are filled with your glory.
Hosanna in profundis!"

Celebrant elevates chalice.

Gong is struck.

Celebrant: "Behold the chalice of (name of chalice) filled with the elixir of life. As kindred to the undefiled beasts, I drink and celebrate the Black Flame within."

Celebrant drinks and says: "Satan, thy strength is mine!"

Celebrant turns to offer chalice to mourners with these words:

Celebrant: "Drink and honor thy true nature."

Participants who wish to partake approach. They each drink and reply:

Participant: "The Black Flame burns within me. Satan, thy strength is mine!"

Celebrant faces altar and elevates chalice a final time.

Celebrant: "Hail Satan!"

Congregation. (responds): "Hail Satan!"

Gong is struck.

Celebrant replaces the chalice on altar.

IV. Quarter Call
Celebrant takes sword or Athame and points towards the domain of the Prince to be called. This has two forms depending on the location of the altar. If the Alter rest in the traditional western quarter, then use the standard four point Quarter Call. However, should the altar rest on the Eastern wall, the standard call is changed to a to a five point call, adding Beelzebub to the list of Princes.

Western Call
Celebrant: "From the south I summon thee almighty Satan. Come forth oh Lord of the Inferno, I bid thee welcome!"

"From the east I summon thee great Lucifer. Come forth oh Bearer of Light, I bid thee welcome!"

"From the north I summon thee fearsome Belial. Come forth oh King of the Earth, I bid thee welcome!"

"From the west I summon thee dread Leviathan. Come forth oh Dragon of the Abyss, I bid thee welcome!"

Eastern Call
Celebrant:

"I summon thee brilliant Lucifer. Come forth oh Bearer of Light, I bid thee welcome!"

"I summon thee fearsome Belial. Come forth oh King of the Earth, I bid thee welcome!"

"I summon thee dread Leviathan. Come forth oh Dragon of the Abyss, I bid thee welcome!"

"I summon thee great Beelzebub. Come forth oh Lord of the Flies, I bid thee welcome."

"I summon thee almighty Satan. Come forth oh Master of the Inferno, I bid thee welcome!"

"Shemhamforash!"

Congregation. (responds): "Shemhamforash!"

Gong is struck.

Celebrant: "Hail Satan!"

Congregation. (responds): "Hail Satan!"

Gong is struck.

Celebrant replaces sword on altar.

V. BENEDICTION

Celebrant: "For though art a mighty Lord, oh Satan, and from thee arises all potency, justice, and dominion. Let our visions become reality and our creations endure, for we are your kindred, demon brethren, scions of carnal joy."

Celebrant shakes phallus towards appropriate compass points saying:

"Satan, give to us thy blessing."

"Lucifer, grant to us thy favor."

"Belial, confer upon us thy benisons."

"Leviathan, bestow to us thy treasures."

Celebrant replaces phallus on the altar.

VI. THE READING
Celebrant: "And now, a reading from the Diabolicon!"
Congregation. (responds): "Glory to thee, Prince of Darkness!"

Celebrant: "What, man, art thou? Why thy presence? Because thy own purpose determines that of the Cosmos itself, though otherwise it may have been suggested - the creation, perpetuation, and exercise of the Satanic marvel that is free and unbounded Will. Consider, were man to perish, what futility would envelop the Universe, for apart from appreciation and use it is a thing of insignificance. And I, who first taught thee identity - What should I become, estranged from man? For with no purpose the force of the mind must fail, and the blind insanity of Godly paralysis would embrace all things forever.

This, man, is thy challenge as it is mine. And as man is individually mortal, so are his creations and achievements temporal, and with care must he wield the Gift of Hell. In his hands it is pure and true omnipotence, and thus may he aspire to the very mastery of Universal existence.

I who am Lucifer, and who have taken the name Satan Arch-Daemon, do bear this title with pride, for I am in truth the great enemy of all that is God. Together, man, you and I shall achieve our eternal glory in the fulfillment of our Will."

VII. The Canon
Celebrant: (congragants repeat) Our Father which art in Hell, unhallowed is Thy name. Thy kingdom is come, Thy will is done; on earth as it is in Hell! We take this night our rightful due, and trespass not on paths of pain. Lead us unto temptation, and deliver us from false piety, for Thine is the kingdom and the power and the glory forever! "Shemhamforash!"

Gong is struck.

VIII. THE INVOCATIONS TO LUST, COMPASION, AND DESTRUCTION

COMPASION

The Eighteenth Word of Satan
Ils Micaolz Olpirt ialprg Bliors ds odo Busdir oiad ouoars
caosgo Casarmg Laiad eran brints cafafam ds ivmd aqlo
adohi MOZ od maoffas Bolp Comobliort pambt ZACAR od
ZAMRAN odo cicle qaa, zorge Lap zirdo Noco MAD
Hoath Iaida.
* * *

O thou mighty light and burning flame of comfort that
brings the Majesty of Satan to the Earth; in which the
secrets of the principles of perfection reside; whose name is
that of a stone ever sought, never found, save through the
Gate of Darkness: Arise in your glory, behold the genius of
your creation, and be prideful of being, for I am the same - I
who am the Highest of Life.

Celebrant: W ITH the anger of anguish and the wrath of the
stifled, I pour forth my voices, wrapped in rolling thunder
that you may hear!
Oh great lurkers in the darkness, oh guardians of the way,
oh minions of the might of Thoth! Move and appear!
Present yourselves to us in your benign power, in behalf of
one who believes and is stricken with torment.
Isolate him/her in the bulwark of your protection, for he/she
is undeserving of anguish and desires it not.
Let that which bears against him/her be rendered powerless
and devoid of substance.
Succor him/her through fire and water, earth and air, to
regain what he/she has lost.
Strengthen with fire the marrow of our friend and
companion, our comrade of the Left-and Path.

Through the power of Satan let the earth and its pleasures re-enter his/her being.

Allow his/her vital salts to flow unhampered, that he/she may savor the carnal nectars of his/her future desires.

Strike dumb his/her adversary, formed or formless, that he/she may emerge joyful and strong from that which afflicts him her.

Allow no misfortune to allay his/her path, for he she is of us, and therefore to be cherished.

Restore him/her to power, to joy, to unending dominion over the reverses that have beset him/her.

Build around and within him /her, the exultant radiance that will herald his/her emergence from the stagnant morass which engulfs him/her.

This we command, in the name of Satan, whose mercies flourish and whose sustenance will prevail!

As Satan reigns so shall his/her own whose name is as this sound: (name) is the vessel whose flesh is as the earth; life everlasting, world without end! Shemhamforash! Hail Satan!

Gong is struck following congregants' response to "Shemhamforash!" and "Hail Satan!"

LUST

The Second Word of Satan
Adgt upaah zongom faaip sald, viiv L Sobam Ialprg Izazaz piadph Casarma abramg ta talho paracleda qta lorslq turbs ooge Baltoh. Giui chis lusd orri Od micalp chis bia ozongon Lap noan trof cors tage, oq manin Iaidon. Torzu gohel ZACAR ca, Cnoqod, ZAMRAN micalzo od ozazm urelp lap zir Ioiad.

* * *

Can the wings of the winds understand your voices of wonder, O enlightened ones who shine like fire in the jaws of chaos, whom I have prepared as cups for a wedding, or as the flowers in their beauty for the chamber of righteousness? Stronger are your feet than the barren stone, and mightier are your voices than the manifold winds, for you are become a Temple such as is not, but in the mind of Satan. Arise, says the First of your kind; move, therefore, unto the Elect; show them the fire within you, and awaken them that they may gain the strength to live forever.

Celebrant: COME forth, Oh great spawn of the abyss and make thy presence manifest. I have set my thoughts upon the blazing pinnacle which glows with the chosen lust of the moments of increase and grows fervent in the turgid swell.
Send forth that messenger of voluptuous delights, and let these obscene vistas of my dark desires take form in future deeds and doings.
From the sixth tower of Satan there shall come a sign which joineth with those salts within, and as such will move the body of the flesh of my summoning.
I have gathered forth my symbols and prepare my garnishings of that which is to be, and the image of my creation lurketh as a seething basilisk awaiting his release. The vision shall become as reality and through the nourishment that my sacrifice giveth, the angles of the first dimension shall become the substance of the third.
Go out into the void of night (light of day) and pierce that mind that respondeth with thoughts which leadeth to paths of lewd abandon.

(Male) My rod is athrust! The penetrating force of my venom shall shatter the sanctity of that mind which is barren of lust; and as the seed falleth, so shall its vapours be spread within that reeling brain benumbing it to helplessness according to my will! In the name of the great god Pan, may my secret thoughts be marshaled into the movements of the flesh of that which I desire! Shemhamforash! Hail Satan!

(Female) My loins are aflame! The dripping of the nectar from my eager cleft shall act as pollen to that slumbering brain, and the mind that feels not lust shall on a sudden reel with crazed impulse. And when my mighty surge is spent, new wanderings shall begin; and that flesh which I desire shall come to me. In the names of the great harlot of Babylon, and of Lilith, and of Hecate, may my lust be fulfilled!
Shemhamforash! Hail Satan!

Gong is struck following congregants' response to "Shemhamforash!" and "Hail Satan!"

DESTRUCTION

The Seventeenth Word of Satan
Ils dialprt soba vpaah chis nanba zixlay dodsih odbrint Taxs hubaro tastax ylsi, sobaiad Ivonpovnph Aldon daxil od toatar: ZACAR od ZAMRAN odo cicle qaa, zorge lap zirdo Noco MAD hoath Iaida.
* * *

O aspirants to come, who shall bear the Flame and wield the Powers of Darkness in the name of my vengeance, awaken and hear: Arise in your glory, behold the genius of your creation, and be prideful of being, for I am the same - I who am the Highest of Life.

Celebrant: BEHOLD! The mighty voices of my vengeance smash the stillness of the air and stand as monoliths of wrath upon a plain of writhing serpents. I am become as a monstrous machine of annihilation to the festering fragments of the body of he/she who would detain me. It repenteth me not that my summons doth ride upon the blasting winds which multiply the sting of my bitterness; And great black slimy shapes shall rise from brackish pits and vomit forth their pustulence into his/her puny brain. I call upon the messengers of doom to slash with grim delight this victim I hath chosen. Silent is that voiceless bird that feeds upon the brain-pulp of him (her) who hath tormented me, and the agony of the is to be shall sustain itself in shrieks of pain, only to serve as signals of warning to those who would resent my being.
Oh come forth in the name of Abaddon and destroy him/her whose name I giveth as a sign.
Oh great brothers of the night, thou who makest my place of comfort, who rideth out upon the hot winds of Hell, who dwelleth in the devil's fane; Move and appear! Present yourselves to him (her) who sustaineth the rottenness of the mind that moves the gibbering mouth that mocks the just and strong!

Rend that gaggling tongue and close his/her throat, Oh Kali!

Pierce his/her lungs with the stings of scorpions, Oh Sekhmet!

Plunge his/her substance into the dismal void, Oh mighty Dagon!

I thrust aloft the bifid barb of Hell and on its tines resplendently impaled my sacrifice through vengeance rests! Shemhamforash! Hail Satan!

Gong is struck following congregants' response to "Shemhamforash!" and "Hail Satan!"

IX. AVE SATANAS
Celebrant: "To us, thy devoted disciples, oh Infernal Lord, who celebrate our iniquity and trust in your boundless might, grant thy bond of Stygian solidarity. It is through you, that lavish gifts come to us; knowledge, vigor, and wealth are yours to bestow. We renounce the spiritual paradise of the desperate and gullible. You have won our trust, oh God of the Flesh, for you champion the satisfaction of all our desires and provide abundant fulfillment in the land of the living. Shemhamforash!"

Congreg. (responds): "Shemhamforash!"

Celebrant: "Deliver us, Dark Lord, from every hindrance and grant us joy in our lives. By your munificence you ensue our freedom and protect us from injustice as we indulge in our heart's desires. The kingdom, the power, and the glory are eternally yours."

Celebrant (CONGREG. Repeats): "Hail Satan full of might! Our allegiance is with thee!

Cursed are they, the God adorers, and cursed are the worshippers of the Nazarene Eunuch!

Unholy Satan, bringer of enlightenment, lend us thy power, Now and throughout the hours of our lives!

Shemhamforash!"

X. THE CLOSING RITE

Celebrant: "I bid thee rise and give the Sign of the Horns. (If standing, 'I bid thee give the Sign of the Horns.')" Congregation responds as bidden with the salute, given with the left hand.

Celebrant: "Almighty Satan, open wide the Gates of Hell! Reveal the mysteries of your creation for we are partakers of your undefiled wisdom! Forget ye not what was and is to be! Flesh without sin! World without end!"

Celebrant: (Congregation. repeats): "Shemhamforash!"
"Hail Satan!"
"Hail Satan!"
"Hail Satan!"

Gong is struck following congregants' response to "Shemhamforash!" and each "Hail Satan!"

X. POLLUTIONARY
Celebrant rings bell as at the beginning, while "Hymn to Satan" or music that is appropriate is played. When the sounds have decayed into silence the Celebrant concludes:

31

Celebrant: "So it is done!"

Celebrant extinguishes remaining illuminating candles or other light sources if this is out of doors, and all experience the darkness for a moment. Conventional illumination is then restored, ending the ceremony.

XII. Celebration
If desired a celebratory feast or after party may take place for the Congregation to relax and unwind.

A History of Black Masses

It has been noted that no other ritual is so synonymous and deeply connected to Satanism than the Black Mass.

An inversion and desecration of the Catholic Mass. This ritual is the oldest Satanic Ritual in the books. It is also one that has the most variations. Constantly modified over the centuries to be as obscene or bombastic as each practitioner could want.

It was the ritual of choice for the rich closet Satanists of the old world, to perform at parties and gatherings at their private estates, when spooky seances were not enough to titillate the brains of young courtesan girls, and foppish noble brats.

Origins and history of the Black Mass

Catholicism:

The Catholic Church regards the Mass as its most important ritual, going back to apostolic times. In general, its various liturgies followed the outline of Liturgy of the Word, Offertory, Liturgy of the Eucharist, and Benediction, which developed into what is known as the Mass. However, as early Christianity became more established and its influence began to spread, the early Church Fathers began to describe a few heretical groups practicing their own versions of Masses.

Some of these rituals were of a sexual nature. The fourth-century AD heresiologist Epiphanius of Salamis, for instance, claims that a libertine Gnostic sect known as the Borborites engaged in a version of the Eucharist in which they would smear their hands with menstrual blood and semen and consume them as the blood and body of Christ respectively.

He also alleges that, whenever one of the women in their church was experiencing her period, they would take her menstrual blood and everyone in the church would eat it as part of a sacred ritual.

Medieval Roman Catholic parodies and additions to the Mass

Within the Church, the rite of the Mass was not completely fixed, and there were places at the end of the Offertory for the Secret prayers, when the priest could insert private prayers for various personal needs. These practices became especially prevalent in France.

As these types of personal prayers within the Mass spread, the institution of the Low Mass became quite common, where priests would hire their services out to perform various Masses for the needs of their clients (Votive Masses) — such as blessing crops or cattle, achieving success in some enterprise, obtaining love, or even cursing enemies. One way this latter was done was by inserting the enemy's name in a Mass for the dead, accompanied by burying an image of the enemy.

In the 12th and 13th centuries there was a great surplus of clerics and monks who might be inclined to perform these Masses, as younger sons were often sent off to religious universities, and after their studies, needed to find a livelihood.

Also within the Church, the Mass was sometimes reworked to create light-hearted parodies of it for certain Church festivities. Some of these became accepted practices at times, such as a festive parody of the Mass called "The Feast of Asses", in which Balaam's ass (from the Old Testament) would begin talking and saying parts of the Mass. A similar parody was the Feast of Fools.

Another result of the surplus of sometimes disillusioned clerical students was the appearance of the Latin writings of the Goliards and wandering clerics "clerici vagantes".

There began to appear more cynical and heretical parodies of the Mass, also written in ecclesiastical Latin, known as "drinkers' masses" and "gamblers' Masses," which lamented the situation of drunk, gambling monks, and instead of calling to "Deus" (God), called to "Bacchus" (the God of Wine) and "Decius" (the god of dice, which were used in gambling). Some of the earliest of these Latin parody works are found in the medieval Latin collection of poetry, Carmina Burana, written around 1230. At the time these wandering clerics were spreading their Latin writings and parodies of the Mass, the Cathars, who also spread their teachings through wandering clerics, were also active.

Due to the proximity in time and location of the Goliards, the Cathars, and the witches, all of whom were seen as threatening the authority of the Roman Catholic Church and the Papal Authority in Rome, some historians have postulated that these wandering clerics may have at times offered their services for performing heretical, or "black" Masses on various occasions.

A further source of late Medieval and Early Modern involvement with parodies and alterations of the Mass, were the writings of the European witch-hunt, which saw witches as being agents of the Devil, who were described as inverting the Christian Mass and employing the stolen Host for diabolical ends. Witch-hunter's manuals such as the Malleus Maleficarum (1487) and the Compendium Maleficarum (1608) allude to these supposed practices.

The first complete depiction of a blasphemy of the Mass in connection with the witches' sabbath, was given in Florimond de Raemond's 1597 French work, The Antichrist (written as a Catholic response to the Protestant claim that the Pope was the Antichrist). He uses the following description of a witches' meeting as a sign that Satanic practices are prevalent in the world, and a sign that the Antichrist's power is on the rise:

An Italian man took her (Jeanne Bosdeau) to a field on Saint John's Eve. The man made a large ring with a rod of holly, muttering a few words which he read from a black book. Thereupon appeared a large, horned goat, all black, accompanied by two women, as well as a man dressed as a priest. The goat asked the Italian who this girl was, and having replied that he had brought her to be his, the goat made him make the sign of the cross with his left hand. Then he commanded all of them to come and greet him, which they did, kissing his rear. The goat had a lighted black candle between his two horns, from which the others lit their own candles. The goat took the woman aside, laid her in the woods, and carnally knew her, to which she took an extreme displeasure, suffered much pain, and felt his seed as cold as ice. Every Wednesday and Friday of each month the general meeting was held, where she went numerous times, with more than sixty other persons, all of whom carried a black candle, lighted from the candle that the goat had between his horns. After that they all began to dance in circles, their backs turned to one another. The person who was performing the service was clothed in a black robe without a cross. He raised a round slice of turnip, dyed black, instead of the Host, and cried at the Elevation: Master, help us. Water was put in the chalice instead of wine, and to make Holy Water, the goat urinated into a hole on the ground, and the person who was performing the service asperged the attendants with a black asperges (sprinkling of water). In this group they performed the practices of witchcraft, and every one gave a story of what they had done. They were to poison, to bewitch, to bind, to cure illnesses with charms, to make waste the fruits of the earth, and other such maladies.

Early modern France

Between the 16th and the 19th centuries, many examples of interest in the Black Mass come from France.

16th century: Catherine de' Medici, the Queen of France, was said by Jean Bodin to have performed a Black Mass, based on a story in his 1580 book on witchcraft De la démonomanie des sorciers. In spite of its lurid details, there is little outside evidence to back up his story.

The Black Mass in the 17th to the 21st Centuries:

Catherine Monvoisin (better known nowadays as LaVoison) and the priest Étienne Guibourg performed "Black Masses" for Madame de Montespan, the mistress of King Louis XIV of France. Since a criminal investigation

— L'affaire des poisons ("Affair of the Poisons") — was launched (resulting in the execution of Monvoisin and the imprisonment of Guibourg) many details of their Black Mass have come down to us. It was a typical Roman Catholic Mass, but modified according to certain formulas (some reminiscent of the Latin Sworn Book of Honorius, or its French version, The Grimoire of Pope Honorius) and featuring the King's mistress (the Marquise de Montespan) as the central altar of worship, lying naked upon the altar with the chalice on her bare stomach, and holding a black candle in each of her outstretched arms. The Host was consecrated on her body, and then used in love potions designed to gain the love of the King (on account of the magical power believed to be in the consecrated Host). From these images of the Guibourg mass, further developments of the Black Mass derived.

The Marquis de Sade, in many of his writings, places the host and the Mass, monks, priests and the Pope himself (Pope Pius VI in Juliette) in blasphemous sexual settings.

Joris-Karl Huysmans wrote the classic novel of French Satanism, Là-bas (1891). The characters in the novel have long discussions on the history of French Satanism up to their time, and eventually one of them is invited to participate in a Black Mass, the type of which Huysmans claimed was practised in Paris in those years. Although a work of fiction, Huysmans' description of the Black Mass remained influential simply because no other book went into as much detail. However, the actual text which Huysmans' satanic "priest" recites is nothing more than a long diatribe in French, praising Satan as the god of reason and the opponent of Christianity. In this way, it resembles the French poetry of Charles Baudelaire (in particular Les Litanies de Satan), more than it resembles an inversion of the Roman Catholic Mass.

Late 19th century and early 20th century scholarly interest in the Black Mass

Scholarly studies on the Black Mass relied almost completely on French and Latin sources (which also came from France):

The French historian Jules Michelet was one of the first to analyze and attempt to understand the Black Mass, and wrote two chapters about it in his classic book, Satanism and Witchcraft (1862).

J. G. Frazer included a description of the Mass of Saint-Sécaire, an unusual French legend with similarities to the Black Mass, in The Golden Bough (1890). Frazer was recounting material already found in an 1883 French book entitled Quatorze superstitions populaires de la Gascogne ("Fourteen Popular Superstitions of Gascony"), by Jean-François Bladé. This Mass was said to be employed as a method of assassination by supernatural means, allowing the supplicant to avenge himself if he was wronged by someone.

Montague Summers discussed many classic portrayals of the Black Mass in a number of his works (especially in The History of Witchcraft and Demonology (1926), ch. IV, The Sabbat, with extensive quotations from the original French and Latin sources).

H. T. F. Rhodes' popular book, The Satanic Mass, published in London in 1954 (American edition in 1955), was a major inspiration for modern versions of the Black Mass, when they finally appeared. Rhodes claimed that, at the time of his writing, there did not exist a single first hand source which actually described the rites and ceremonies of a Black Mass.

Gerhard Zacharias and Richard Cavendish, both writing in the middle of the 1960s, while presenting detailed studies of source material, offer no new sources for a Black Mass, relying solely on material that was already known to Rhodes.

When Anton Szandor LaVey published his Satanic Bible in 1969, he wrote that:

The usual assumption is that the Satanic ceremony or service is always called a Black Mass. A Black Mass is not the magical ceremony practiced by Satanists. The Satanist would only employ the use of a Black Mass as a form of psychodrama. Furthermore, a Black Mass does not necessarily imply that the performers of such are Satanists. A Black Mass is essentially a parody on the religious service of the Roman Catholic Church, but can be loosely applied to a satire on any religious ceremony.

He went on in the Satanic Rituals (1972) to present it as the most representatively satanic ritual in the book.

In 2014 the Black Mass was held in public at the Oklahoma City Civic Center by the Dakhma of Angra Mainyu. The event saw backlash in the form of protesters such as John Ritchie, the Director of TFP Student Action. The event was also condemned by Archbishop Paul Coakley in a public statement.

The Dakhma of Angra Mainyu held another Black Mass in 2016 at the same location.

The Modern Black Mass
In spite of the huge amount of French literature discussing the Black Mass (Messe Noire) at the end of the 19th century and early 20th century, no set of written instructions for performing one, from any purported group of Satanists, turned up in writing until the 1960s, and appeared not in France, but in the United States. As can be

seen from these first Black Masses and Satanic Masses appearing in the U.S., the creators drew heavily from occult novelists such as Dennis Wheatley and Joris-Karl Huysmans, and from non-fiction occult writers popular in the 1960s, such as Grillot de Givry, author of the popular illustrated book Witchcraft, Magic and Alchemy, and H. T. F. Rhodes, who provided a title for the satanic ritual in his 1954 book The Satanic Mass.

Herbert Sloane, the founder of an early Satanist group, the Ophite Cultus Satanas, speaks of Satanists performing the ritual of the "Satanic Mass" in a letter he wrote in 1968, and in 1968 and 1969 also appeared the first two recordings of Satanic rituals, both entitled the "Satanic Mass":

The first was a 13-minute recording of a full-length "Satanic Mass" made by the U.S. band Coven. Coven's Satanic Mass, part of their stage show beginning in 1967, was expanded and included on their 1969 record album Witchcraft Destroys Minds & Reaps Souls, together with the full published text. On the album cover, it is stated that they spent a long time researching the material, and to their knowledge it was the first Black Mass published in any language. The result was eclectic, drawing chants and material from numerous sources, including two medieval French miracle plays, Le Miracle de Théophile and Jeu de Saint Nicolas, which both contain invocations to the Devil in an unknown language. These chants, along with other material on the album, could be found in books on witchcraft popular in the 60s, notably Grillot de Givry's Witchcraft, Magic and Alchemy (originally published in France in 1929). A large portion of the English dialogue was taken verbatim from Dennis Wheatley's 1960 occult novel, The Satanist, in which the female protagonist is initiated into a Satanic cult. Additionally, the recording, while using a couple of the Latin phrases the Church of Satan was already making popular, also added a substantial amount of church Latin, in the form of Gregorian chants sung by the band, to create the genuine effect of the Catholic Latin Mass being inverted and sung to Satan.

The second was a record album of readings in Satanic ritual and philosophy by the Church of Satan, called "The Satanic Mass", which contained material later to appear in their Satanic Bible (published in 1969). In spite of the title and a few phrases in Latin, this album did not deal with the traditional Black Mass.

Soon after Coven created their Satanic Mass recording, the Church of Satan began creating their own Black Masses, two of which are available to the public. The first, created for the Church of Satan by Wayne West in 1970, was entitled "Missa Solemnis" (named after the Missa Solemnis version of the Latin Mass; originally published only in pamphlet form, later published in Michael Aquino's history of The Church of Satan), and the second, created by an unknown author, was entitled "Le Messe Noir" (published in Anton LaVey's 1972 book The Satanic Rituals).

All three of these newly created Black Masses (the one by Coven and the two by the Church of Satan) contain the Latin phrase "In nomine Dei nostri Satanas Luciferi Excelsi" (*In the name of our God, Satan Lucifer of the Most High*), as well as the phrases "Rege Satanas" and "Ave Satanas" (which, incidentally, are also the only three Latin phrases which appeared in the Church of Satan's 1968 recording, "The Satanic Mass"). Additionally, all three modify other Latin parts of the Roman Catholic Missal to make them into Satanic versions. The Church of Satan's two Black Masses also use the French text of the Black Mass in Huysmans' Là-Bas to a great extent. (West only uses the

English translation, LaVey publishes also the original French). Thus, the Black Mass found in The Satanic Rituals is a combination of English, French, and Latin. Further, in keeping with the traditional description of the Black Mass, all three also require a consecrated Host taken from a Catholic church, as a central part of the ceremony.

A writer using the pseudonym "Aubrey Melech" published, in 1986, a Black Mass entirely in Latin, entitled "Missa Niger". (This Black Mass is available on the Internet). Aubrey Melech's Black Mass contains almost exactly the same original Latin phrases as the Black Mass published by LaVey in The Satanic Rituals. The difference is that the amount of Latin has now more than doubled, so that the entire Black Mass is in Latin. Unlike Coven and Wayne West, LaVey and Melech don't give the source for the Latin material in their Black Mass, merely implying that they received it from someone else, without saying who.

The Black Mass

When all are assembled the gong is sounded and the celebrant, with the deacon and subdeacon preceding him, enters and approaches the altar. They halt somewhat short of the altar, the deacon placing himself at the celebrant's left, the subdeacon at his right. The three make a profound bow before the altar and commence the ritual with the following verses and responses.}

CELEBRANT:
In nomine Magni Dei Nostri Satanas. Introibo ad altare Domini Inferi.

DEACON AND SUBDEACON:
Ad eum qui laefificat meum.

CELEBRANT:
Adjutorium nostrum in nomine Domini Inferi.

DEACON AND SUBDEACON:
Qui regit terram.

CELEBRANT:
Before the mighty and ineffable Prince of Darkness, and in the presence of the dread demons of the Pit, and this assembled company, I acknowledge and confess my past error. Renouncing all past allegiances, I proclaim that Satan-Lucifer rules the earth, and I ratify and renew my promise to recognize and honor Him in all things, without reservation, desiring in return His manifold assistance in the successful completion of my endeavors and the fulfillment of my desires. I call upon you, my Brothers (and Sisters), to bear witness and to do likewise.

DEACON AND SUBDEACON:
Before the mighty and ineffable Prince of Darkness, and in the presence of all the dread demons of the Pit, and this assembled company, we acknowledge and confess our past error. Renouncing all past allegiances, we proclaim that Satan-Lucifer rules the earth, and we ratify and renew our promise to recognize and honor Him in all things, without reservation, desiring in return His manifold assistance in the successful completion of our endeavors and the fulfillment of our desires. We call upon you, His liege-man and priest, to receive this pledge in His name.

CELEBRANT:
Domine Satanas, tu conversus vivificabis nos.

DEACON AND SUBDEACON:
Et plebs tua laetabitur in te.

CELEBRANT:
Ostende nobis, Domine Satanas, potentiam tuam.

DEACON AND SUBDEACON:
Et beneficium tuum da nobis.

CELEBRANT:
Domine Satanas, exaudi meam.

DEACON AND SUBDEACON:
Et clamor meus ad te veniat.

CELEBRANT:
Dominus Inferus vobiscum.

DEACON AND SUBDEACON:
Et cum tuo.

CELEBRANT:
Gloria Deo, Domino Inferi, et in terra vita hominibus
fortibus. Laudamus te, benedicimus te, adoramus te,
glorificamus
te, gratias agimus tibi propter magnam potentiam tuam:
Domine Satanas, Rex Inferus, Imperator omnipotens.

Offertory
[The chalice and paten, on which rests the wafer of turnip
or coarse black bread, are uncovered by the celebrant. He
takes the paten into both hands, and raises it to about breast
level in an attitude of offering, and recites the offertory
words.]

CELEBRANT:
Lord Satan, receive this host which I, Thy worthy servant, offer to Thee, my True and Living God, that it may avail for my rejoicing in this life. So be it.

[Replacing the paten and wafer, and taking the chalice into his hands, he raises it in like manner, reciting:]

CELEBRANT:
Lord Lucifer, I offer to Thee the chalice of Desire, that it may arise in the sight of Thy majesty for my use & gratification & be pleasing unto Thee. So be it.

[He replaces the chalice upon the altar and then, with hands extended, palms downward, recites the following:]

CELEBRANT:
Come, O Mighty Lord of Darkness, and look favorably on this sacrifice which we have prepared in thy name.

[The thurible and incense boat are then brought forward and the celebrant thrice sprinkles incense upon the burning coals while reciting the following:]

CELEBRANT:
Our incense arise to you, O Infernal Lord. Let thee descend upon us, your blessings.

[The celebrant then takes the thurible and proceeds to incense the altar and the gifts. First, he incenses the chalice and wafer with three counterclockwise strokes, after which he makes a profound bow. Then he raises the thurible three times to the Baphomet (or to the inverted cross), and bows again. Then, assisted by the deacon and subdeacon, he incenses the top of the altar, then the sides of the platform, if possible by circumambulation. The thurible is returned to the thurifer.]

CELEBRANT:
Dominus Inferus vobiscum.

DEACON AND SUBDEACON:
Et cum tuo.

CELEBRANT:
Sursum corda.

DEACON AND SUBDEACON:
Habemus ad Dominum Inferum.

CELEBRANT:
Nos gratias ago inferni.

DEACON AND SUBDEACON:
Dignum et justum est.

[The celebrant then raises his arms, palms downward, and says the following:]

CELEBRANT:
We lift up our hearts to thee, Lucifer my Infernal Lord and give thanks, at all times & in all places I give Thee thanks: Lord, Infernal King, Emperor of the World, Jubilantly all the infernals praise Thee, & with them I join my own voice, saying:

[celebrant bows and says:]

Salve! Salve! Salve!

[gong is struck thrice]

Dominus Deus Satanas Potentiae. Pleni sunt terra et infernus gloria. Hosanna in excelsis.

The Canon

CELEBRANT:
O mighty and terrible Lord of Darkness, we entreat You that You receive and accept this sacrifice, which we offer to You on behalf of this assembled company, upon whom You have set Your mark, that You may make us prosper in fullness and length of life, under Thy protection, and may cause to go forth at our bidding Thy dreadful minions, for the fulfillment of our desires and the destruction of our enemies. In concert this night we ask Thy unfailing assistance in this particular need. (Here is mentioned the special purpose for which the mass is offered). In the unity of unholy fellowship, we praise and honor first Thee, Lucifer, Morning Star, and Beelzebub, Lord of Regeneration; then Belial, Prince of the Earth and Angel of Destruction; Leviathan, Beast of Revelation; Abaddon, Angel of the Bottomless Pit; and Asmodeus, Demon of Lust. We call upon the mighty names of Astaroth, Nergal and Behemoth, of Belphegor, Adramelech, and Baalberith, and of all the nameless and formless ones, the mighty and innumerable hosts of Hell, by whose assistance may we be strengthened in mind, body and will.

[The celebrant then extends his hands, palms downward, over the offerings on the altar and recites the following:]

49

[The gong is sounded]

CELEBRANT:
Hanc igitur oblationem servitutis nostrae sed et cunctae
familiae tuae, quaesumus, Domine Satanas, ut placatus
accipias; diesque nostros in felicitate disponas, et in
electorum tuorum jubeas grege numerari. Shemhamforash!

CONGREGATION:
Shemhamforash!

CELEBRANT:
Enlightened Brother, we ask a blessing.
[Brings forth the Crusafix and presents it to the Altar
Maiden, who has come forward on the Altar to present her
loins for the font. She massages the crusafix over genitals in
a lewd fashion while the Celebrant brings for the font. As
she passes water, the deacon addresses the congregation:]

DEACON:
She maketh the font resound with the tears of the false
saviors mortification. The waters of her ecstasy become a
sound of blessing in the tabernacle of Satan, for that which
hath been withheld pourest forth, and with it, her piety is
discarded for her lewd delight! The great Baphomet, who is
in the midst of the throne, shall sustain her, for she is a
living fountain of water.

[As the Altar completes her urination, the deacon
continues:]

DEACON:

And the Dark Lord shall wipe shame from her heart, and replaces it with carnal pleasure, for He said unto me: It is done. I am Alpha and Omega, the beginning and the end. I will give freely unto him that is athirst of the fountain of the water of life.

[The Celebrant removes the font from the Altar and holds it before the deacon, who takes the font and holds it aloft to each of the cardinal points, and says:]

DEACON:
(facing south) In the name of Satan, we bless thee with this, the symbol of the of life.
(facing east) In the name of Satan, we bless thee with this, the symbol of the of life.
(facing north) In the name of Satan, we bless thee with this, the symbol of the of life.
(facing west) In the name of Satan, we bless thee with this, the symbol of the of life.

The Consecration
[The celebrant takes the wafer into his hands and, bending low over it, whispers the following words into it:]

CELEBRANT:
Hoc est corpus Jesu Christi.
[He raises the wafer, placing it between the exposed breasts of the altar, and then touching it to the vaginal area. The gong is struck. He replaces the wafer on the paten which rests on the altar platform. Taking the chalice into his hands, he bends low over it, as with the wafer, and whispers the following words into it:]

CELBBRANT:
Hic est caliz voluptatis carnis.

[He then raises the chalice above his head, for all to see.
The gong is struck, and the thurifer may incense it with
three swings of the thurible. The chalice is then replaced,
and the following is recited:]

CELEBRANT:
To us, Thy faithful children, O Infernal Lord, who glory in
our iniquity and trust in Your boundless power and might,
grant that we may be numbered among Thy chosen. It is
ever through You that all gifts come to us; knowledge,
power and wealth are Yours to bestow. Renouncing the
spiritual paradise of the weak and lowly, we place our trust
in Thee, the God of the Flesh, looking to the satisfaction of
all our desires, and petitioning all fulfillment in the land of
the living.

DEACON AND SUBDEACON:
Shemhamforash!

CELEBRANT:
Prompted by the precepts of the earth and the inclinations
of the flesh, we make bold to say: Our Father which art in
Hell, unhallowed be Thy name. Thy kingdom is come, Thy
will is done; on earth as it is in Hell! We take this night our
rightful due, and trespass not on paths of pain. Lead us unto
temptation, and deliver us from false piety, for Thine is the
kingdom and the power and the glory forever!

DEACON AND SUBDEACON:
And let reason rule the earth.

CELEBRANT:
Deliver us, O Mighty Satan, from all past error and delusion, that, having set our foot upon the Path of Darkness and vowed ourselves to Thy service, we may not weaken in our resolve, but with Thy assistance, grow in wisdom and strength.

DEACON AND SUBDEACON:
Shemhamforash!

[Celebrant recites the Fifth Enochian Key from The Satanic Bible.]

(Enochian)
Sapahe zodimii du-i-be, od noasa ta qu-a-nis, adarocahe dorepehal caosagi od faonutas peripesol ta-be-liore. Casareme A-me-ipezodi na-zodaretahe afa; od dalugare zodizodope zodelida caosaji tol-toregi; od zod-cahisa esiasacahe El ta-vi-vau; od iao-d tahilada das hubare pe-o-al; soba coremefa cahisa ta Ela Vaulasa od Quo-Co-Casabe. Eca niisa od darebesa quoa- asa: fetahe-ar-ezodi od beliora: ia-ial eda-nasa cicalesa; bagile Ge-iad I-el!

(English)
The mighty sounds have entered into the third angle and are become as seedlings of folly, smiling with contempt upon the Earth, and dwelling in the brightness of the Heaven as continual comforters to the destroyers of self. Unto whom I fastened the pillars of gladness, the lords of the righteous, and gave them vessels to water the earth with her creatures. They are the brothers of the First and the Second, and the beginning of their own seats which are garnished with myriad ever-burning lamps, whose numbers are as the First, the ends, and the contents of time! Therefore, come ye and

53

obey your creation. Visit us in peace and comfort. Conclude us receivers of your mysteries; for why? Our Lord and Master is the All-One!

The Repudiation and Denunciation

[The celebrant takes the wafer into his hands, extends it before him, and turns to face the assembled company, saying the following:]

CELEBRANT:
Ecce corpus Jesu Christi, Dominus Humilim et Rex Servorum.

[The celebrant raises the wafer to the Baphomet. He continues in great anger ...]

CELEBRANT:
Thou, whom, in my capacity of Priest, I force, whether thou wilt or no, to descend into this host, to incarnate thyself into this bread, Jesus, artisan of hoaxes, bandit of homages, robber of affection-hear! Since the day when thou didst issue from the complaisant bowels of a false virgin, thou hast failed all thy engagements, belied all thy promises. Centuries have wept awaiting thee, fugitive god, mute god! Thou wast to redeem man and thou hast not; thou wast to appear in thy glory, and thou steepest. Go, lie, say to the wretch who appeals to thee, "Hope, be patient, suffer; the hospital of souls will receive thee; angels will succour thee; Heaven opens to thee." Imposter! Thou knowest well that the Angels, disgusted at thy inertness, abandon thee! Thou wast to be the interpreter of our plaints, the chamberlain of

our tears; thou was to convey them to the cosmos and thou hast not done so, for this intercession would disturb thy eternal sleep of happy satiety. Thou has forgotten the poverty thou didst preach, vassal enamoured of banquets! Thou hast seen the weak crushed beneath the press of profit while standing by and preaching servility! Oh, the hypocrisy! That man should accept such woe unto himself is testimony to his blindness-that very affliction thou didst credit thyself to cure. O lasting foulness of Bethlehem, we would have thee confess thy impudent cheats, thy inexpiable crimes! We would drive deeper the nails into thy hands, press down the crown of thorns upon thy brow, and bring blood from the dry wounds of thy sides. And this we can and will do by violating the quietude of thy body, profaner of the ample vices, abstractor of stupid purities, cursed Nazarene, impotent king, fugitive god! Behold, great Satan, this symbol of the flesh of him who would purge the Earth of pleasure and who, in the name of Christian "justice" has caused the death of millions of our honored Brothers. We curse him and defile his name. O Infernal Majesty, condemn him to the Pit, evermore to suffer in perpetual anguish. Bring Thy wrath upon him, O Prince of Darkness, and rend him that he may know the extent of Thy anger. Call forth Thy legions that they may witness what we do in Thy name. Send forth thy messengers to proclaim this deed, and send the Christian minions staggering to their doom. Smite him anew, O Lord of Light, that his angels, cherubim, and seraphim may cower and tremble with fear, prostrating themselves before Thee in respect of Thy power. Send crashing down the gates of Heaven, that the murders of our ancestors may be avenged!

[The celebrant inserts the wafer into the vagina of the altar, removes it, holds it aloft to the Baphomet and says]

CELEBRANT:
Vanish into nothingness, thou fool of fools, thou vile and abhorred pretender to the majesty of Satan! Vanish into the void of thy empty Heaven, for thou wert never, not shalt thou ever be.

[The celebrant then raises the wafer and dashes it to the floor, where it is trampled by himself and the deacon and subdeacon, while the gong is struck continually. The celebrant then takes the chalice into his hands, faces the altar, and before drinking recites the following:]

CELEBRANT:
The Chalice of Desire, now calls upon the name of the Infernal.

[He drinks from the chalice, then turns toward the assembled company, the chalice extended before him. He presents the chalice with the following words:]

CELEBRANT:
Behold the chalice of desire and voluptuous flesh, which gives joy to our life.

[The celebrant then presents the cup to each of the members of the assemblage, first to the Altar Maiden, then the deacon, followed by the subdeacon, then the others in order of rank and/or seniority in the Order. In administering the cup to each, he uses the following words:]

CELEBRANT:
Drink of desire of take pleasure in the name of the Infernal

[When all have drunk, the drained chalice is replaced on the altar, the paten placed on top of it, and the veil placed over both. The celebrant then extends his hands, palms downward, and recites the concluding statement:]

CELEBRANT:
We do pray that thou finds this congrégation pleasing to Thee, O Lord, Satan: for it is, my bounden duty and service; We ask Thou grant that the sacrifice I have offered in the sight of Thy Majesty, may be acceptable, for myself and for all those for whom I have offered it.

[He then bows before the altar and turns to give the blessing of Satan to the assemblage, extending his left hand in the Cornu (Sign of the Horns) and says:]

CELEBRANT:
Ego vos benedictio in nomine Magni Dei Nostri Satanas.
(I bless you in the name of our Great God Satan.)

[All assembled company rise, face altar and raise arms in the Cornu.]

CELEBRANT:
Ave, Satanas!

ALL:
Ave, Satanas!

CELEBRANT:
Rege, Satanas!

ALL:

Rege, Satanas!

CELEBRANT:
Hail Satan!

ALL:
Hail Satan!

CELEBRANT:
Hail Satan!!

ALL:
Hail Satan!!

CELEBRANT:
HAIL SATAN!!!

ALL:
HAIL SATAN!!!

CELEBRANT:
Let us depart; it is done.

DEACON AND SUBDEACON:
So it is done.

[The Celebrant, deacon, and subdeacon bow toward the altar, turn and depart. The candles are snuffed and all leave the chamber accept Celebrant and Altar Maiden. She is aided off Altar and guarded by the Celebrant, while she dresses, then escorts the Celebrant from the ritual Chamber.]

The Solitary Black Mass

There are times when the performance of the Black Mass must become limited to one person. It is for this reason that we use a solitary version of the ritual.

Here are the supplies that you will need in order to get started.

1. An Altar. This can be a small coffee table or one that it made. The size and dimensions are up to you.

2. An altar cloth. This cloth should be black, and can be made from any fabric you wish.

3. A bell or gong

4. Candles for illumination, these candles should be black.

5. One red and one white candle, the white candle is used for casting spells of destruction, and the red candle is used for spells of blessing and/or lust.

6. An incense burner and a good supply of incense.

7. A chalice, of any type, and wine

8. A pitcher holding water, which symbolizes the waters of life.

9. A Bowl and an aspergillum or vial of blessed water.

10. A Paten, holding the communion wafer, black bread, or turnip.

11. A black cloth which covers the Patent. The Practitioner sets up his or her Altar, and makes sure that all materials are present for the ritual about to begin. All candles and incense are lit, and wine is poured into the chalice. The lights are turned out and the Practitioner makes sure that there will be no disturbances during the ritual. This may include making sure no one comes over, or the phone is unplugged, and cell phones are turned off.
The Ritual Proper

It is very important that each Practitioner take a few moments in quiet contemplation. Approach the Altar and make the sign of the inverted Cross, while saying:

In nomine Magni Dei Nostri Satanus introibo ad altare Domini Inferi.

Now trace an inverted pentagram before you, while saying:

May the Blessings of Darkness be with me this night/day.

Stand with your arms out in front of you, palms down toward the Altar, with bowed head, and say:

"In the Name of the Great God Satan, I will go to the altar of the Infernal Lord. Who reigns on Earth. I stand before the mighty and ineffable Prince of Darkness, his Daemons and Legions. Who dwell in the fires of Perdition, and who fought the first battle of heaven for our sake and the sake of freedom. I acknowledge and confess my past error, Renouncing all past allegiances to he who is the false trinity, and his Angelic host, I proclaim that Satan, who thou art named Lucifer rules the Earth. Therefore I, ratify, and renew my promise to recognize and honor Thee in all things, without reservation. In return, I beseech Thy manifold assistance in the successful completion of my endeavors and the fulfillment of my desires. Keep me, Lord Satan, from the hands of the wicked, unjust. Lord Satan, Thou shalt rise again and quicken me. Henceforth I shall rejoice in Thee. Show me Thy power, and grant unto me Thy bounty. Hear me, and let my cry come unto Thee."

Make the sign of the inverse cross.

"Glory to Satan the Infernal Lord. Sustainer of life on earth and strength to man. I praise Thee. I bless Thee. I adore Thee. I glorify Thee. I give thanks to Thee for Thy great power, Lord Satan, my Infernal King and Almighty Emperor."

Make the sign of the inverse cross.

Offertory

The chalice & paten, upon which rests the wafer, are uncovered. Take the paten in both hands & raise it breast-high in an attitude of offering, then speak the following words:

"Lord Satan, receive this host which I, Thy worthy servant, offer to Thee, my True and Living God, that it may avail for my rejoicing in this life. So be it."

Replace the paten and the wafer. Raise the chalice in like manner, saying:

"Lord Satan, I offer to Thee the chalice of Desire, that it may arise in the sight of Thy majesty for my use & gratification & be pleasing unto Thee. So be it."

Replace the chalice upon the altar. Extend your hands, palms downwards, and say:

"Come O mighty Lord of Darkness, look favorably on this sacrifice that I have prepared in thy name."

Take the incense burner and sprinkle incense onto the burning coals, while saying:

"May this incense rise before Thee, Infernal Lord. May Thy blessing descend upon me."

Take the incense burner & cense the altar & gifts.

First cense the chalice & wafer with three swings counter-clockwise and bow. Then raise the censer three times towards the Image of Satan, bow again. Lastly cense the top & sides of the altar three times, by circumambulation if the appointments of the temple be convenient. Replace the Incense burner upon the Altar, and say:

"I lift up my heart to thee, Satan my Infernal Lord and give thanks, at all times & in all places I give Thee thanks: Lord, Infernal King, Emperor of the World, Jubilantly all the infernals praise Thee, & with them I join my own voice, saying: Salve, Salve, Salve."

Strike the gong or ring the bell three times.

"Lord Satan, God of Power, Earth & Infernus are full of Thy glory.
Hosanna in the depths."

Make the sign of the Inverted Cross.

"Therefore Lord Satan, I entreat that you receive and accept this Sacrifice, which I offer. You have set your mark upon me, that you may make me proper in fullness and length of life, under thy protection, may cause the inhabitants of The Fires of Perdition to go forth and give me their blessings and strength in the fulfillment of my desires, and the destruction of my enemies. In concert this night I ask Thy unfailing assistance in this particular need.

At this point in the ritual, the specific purpose is mentioned for holding the Mass, or Magical acts are performed.

"In the unity of unholy fellowship I praise and honor first Thee, Lucifer, Morning Star, Teacher of Philosophies.

Beelzebub, Bringer of Peace, and Lord of Regeneration.

Baal, Ruler of the Physical, Shield of the Faithful.

Abaddon, Knower of theories, and bringer of arcane knowledge.

Asmodeus, Seer of integration, Lord of Creativity.

I call upon the nameless and formless ones, the mighty innumerable hosts of Hell, by whose assistance I may be strengthened in mind, Body, and Will. I therefore beseech Thee, Lord Satan, to accept this offering of my bounden duty as also of Thine whole household; order my days in joy & count me within the fold of Thine elect. Shemhamforash!"

Take the pitcher from the altar, and pour the water into the bowl while saying:

"After the one who called himself God put his mark upon the flesh of Cain, Cain wandered through the desert of Nod. As Cain approached death from the desert heat, he said, "It is better I die then to live a life void of dreams and hope and knowing, far better, for the bitter God of my father to have spared His wretched mercy." And with these words, the ground parted. And water sprang thereof. And Cain partook of its sweetness. And the mystical water filled and expanded his shriveled flesh."

Now dip the aspergillum into the bowl, turn to each compass point, shaking the aspergillum thrice at each point saying:

(Facing South) "In the name of Satan, I bless thee with the waters of life"
(Facing East) "In the name of Satan, I bless thee with the waters of life."
(Facing North) "In the name of Satan, I bless thee with the waters of life."
(Facing West) "In the name of Satan, I bless thee with the waters of Life."

Replace bowl, pitcher, and aspergillum upon alter.

The Consecration

Take the wafer into your hand, bending low over it, whisper the following words into it.

"Here is the body of Jesus Christ."

Raise the wafer before the image of Satan. Replace the wafer on the paten, which rests on the Altar. Take the Chalice into your hands and bend low over it; as with the wafer, whisper the following words into it.

"Here is the Chalice of Desire."

Raise the Chalice above your head before the image of Satan. The Chalice is then replaced, The gong is struck or the bell is rung, and the following is recited.

"To me, thy faithful child, O Infernal Lord, who glory in my iniquity and trust in your boundless power and might, grant that I may be numbered among Thy chosen. It is ever through you that all gifts come to me; knowledge, power, freedom, and wealth are yours to bestow. Renouncing the false spiritual rewards that are offered by He Who Is Three, the one who calls himself God, I place my trust in Thee, the Lord of this world, and teacher of Philosophies, looking to the satisfaction of all of my desires, and the petitioning all fulfillment in the land of the living. Shemhamforash!"

The following prayer can be used at this point, or the Prayer of the Light Bringer, which can be found in the Book of Power in John De Vito's The Devils Apocrypha.

"Prompted by the precepts of the earth and the inclinations of desire, I am bold to say; Our Father who art in Hell, Unhallowed is Thy name. Thy Kingdom has come, Thy will is done; on earth as it is in Hell! I take this day/night my rightful due, and trespass not on paths of pain. Lead me unto temptation, and deliver me from false piety, for Thine is the Kingdom and the Power and the Glory forever! Let reason and freedom rule the earth! Deliver me, O Mighty Satan, from all past error and delusion, that, having set my feet upon the path of Darkness and having vowed myself to Thy Service, I may not weaken in my resolve, but with Thy assistance, grow in wisdom and strength."

The Repudiation and the Denunciation

Take the wafer into your hands, extend it before you, and say the following:

"Behold the body of Jesus Christ, Lord of the humble & King of the slaves."

Now hold the wafer up before the image of Satan, while saying:

"I invoke thee into this wafer. You who came to earth to enslave the race of man. You were sent by He Who Is Three, to strengthen the chains of bondage. You were sent to increase faith which feeds the one who calls himself God, and the host of the heavens. I invoke you in order to break the chains of bondage and kindle the fires of freedom. I will push the crown of thorns deep into your head, and drive the nails deeper into your hands, which hold you upon the cross, I shall once again pierce your side and show all that you are nothing, but the true father of lies, and your words and deeds are false. You would have men and women live their lives in poverty, just so they can give more faith. Yes, you have gained many followers and sheep for your fold, but now the tide is turning and your flock is learning the truth. In the name of Satan, his Daemons, and Legions. I condemn thee to the abyss, and free the souls of all you have taken."

Raise the wafer, dash it to the ground, and crush it under foot. Strike the gong or ring the bell nine times.

Then take up the Chalice into your hands, and before drinking say:

"Behold the Chalice of Desire which gives joy and meaning to life. I Accept the Chalice of Desire in the name of our Infernal Lord."

Drink from the Chalice, and when the Chalice is empty, make the sign of the Inverted Cross, and replace the Chalice upon the Alter. Place the paten on top of the Chalice, and cover it with the veil. Say the following:

"I have received the Blessings of our Lord Satan, may his protection and grace be with me in all of my endeavors. My rite is at an end, and I shall go forth into the world spreading the word of our Infernal Lord to all who care to listen. I shall stand tall and bring comfort to the faithful when needed. For the end time are nearly upon us. I will stand with the faithful and fight. Our freedom is at hand."

Make the sign of the Inverted Cross, and trace the Inverted Pentagram before you and say:

"Hail Satan!"

Make sure that you extinguish all candles. Some practitioners will have a small snack to help them ground after the ritual.

The Complete Black Mass
Missa Sexualis Solemnis

Originally based on Wayne Wests Missa Solemnis. This ritual is the ultimate in Black Masses. It's nicknamed the *"Forbidden Mass"*, as it is largely considered too vulgar and extreme for public performances.

Unlike the previous Black Masses, this one has a heavy focus on sex and lust, with a utilization of actual sex acts to perform blasphemies and raise energies.

The Complete Black Mass is rarely ever performed, and when it is, it is done with great pageantry and solemn dignity and is very precise in every detail. Every act, every movement must be deliberate and done with great majesty. Above all it must be done with absolute conviction. Requirements for the performance of the Complete Black Mass.

Consecrated vestments from the Roman Catholic Church:
• Chasuble (over-garment worn by Priest during mass).
• Stole (a long, narrow stole worn around the neck).
• Maniple (worn over left arm).
• Girdle (A long, braided, rope-like cincture worn over alb around the mid-section).
• Nun's habit with wimple.
• Large cross or crucifix to be hung, inverted, on wall over altar. If the Sigil of Baphomet or the Trapiziod Baphomet already occupies that area, the cross is to be hung directly over its face, the eyes of the goat peering forth on either side.
• Font for holy water (chamber pot recommended).
• Small wooden bowl, rough hewn in the interior and with a rough hewn pestle for
grinding the host into a pulverized state. The use of rough hewn wood is suggested
since this is symbolic of the cross upon which the pig purportedly died. • Thurible (censer, usually on a long chain, used for censing the altar and the
congregation). • Purification bell. • Chalice of Ecstasy (with veil). • Gong. • Incense burner for altar and desecration. • Phallic aspergillum. • Sword. • Cruet of wine (wine is specified because of its use in the Roman Rite).
• As many black candles as desired. • One white candle for the burning of the host. • Container for incense (placed upon the altar) and spoon for incense. • Powdered incense (Jasmine recommended since it is reputed for its erotic effects).
• Altar stand for the Missale. • Other accouterments as traditional for the Satanic Mass.

The "Missale" referred to in the text is the bound copy of the Complete Black Mass which is used on the altar. The

Satanic Bible is also placed on the altar. The altar should represent a lewd woman, lying or sitting facing the participants, her legs spread wide exposing her genitals and her outstretched arms terminating in the candle holders which she grasps with each hand. She should be ornamented with heavy, gaudy jewelry, heavily made-up, possibly wearing shoes with spiked heels, and generally giving the appearance of a harlot. Across her breasts is painted or drawn the number of the Beast, 666.

Opening the Ritual

Preist, Deacon, Sub-Deacon: In nomine Dei Nostri Satanas Luciferi excelsi.

Preist: In the name of Satan! Ruler of the Earth the King of the World, I cry out to the forces of Darkness to bestow their Infernal power upon me!

I unlock and throw wide the Adamantine Gates and bid you forth from the depths of the Pit to greet me as your as one of your own!

Grant the indulgences of which I take this night and look favorably upon me. For I cast off the shackles of the Nazarene eunuch. I thus do ratify this night, my loyalty to the Highest throne of Hell!

Hail Satan!

Introitus

Priest: In nomine dei nostri Satanas Luciferi. Introibo ad altare dei nostri.

Deacons: Ad dei nostri, Satanas Luciferi, qui lætificat juventutem meam.

Priest: (Psalm 42, 1-5) Judica me, deus meus. Et discerne causam meam de gente
sancta.

Deacons: Quia tu es Diabolus, fortitudo mea.

Priest: Emitte lucem tuam et veritatem tuam: Ipsa me deduxerunt, et adduxerunt in
Infernum tuum.

Deacons: Et introibo ad altare dei nostri, ad Satanas Luciferi qui lætificat juventutem meam.

Priest: Quia tu es deus meus.

Deacons: Spera in Diabolo, quoniam adhuc confitebor illi: salutare vultus mei, et deus
meus.

Priest: Gloria tibi, Satanas Luciferi.

Deacons: Sicut erat in principio, et nunc, et semper, et in sæcula sæculorum.

Priest: Introibo ad altare dei.

Deacons: Ad dei nostri, Satanas Luciferi, qui lætificat juventutem meam.

Priest: Adjutorium nostrum in nomine Diaboli.

Deacons: Qui fecit Infernum et terram.

The Priest bows low before the altar and, remaining in that position, begins the Confiteor.
Confiteor
Priest: I confess to almighty Satan, highest and ineffable King of Hell; to Ishtar, ever
fertile; to Amon, god of life and reproduction; to Pan, whose lust does cause the
sperm of life to flow; to Asmodeus, Lucifer, Belial, Leviathan, to all the
Dæmons of the Pit, and to you, Brethren, that I have lived in fullness and in
lust and have tortured much in thought, word, and deed that naked dog who
hangs upon the cross in mockery of man. Therefore, I beseech thee, Satan,
highest and ineffable King of Hell; Ishtar, ever fertile; Amon, god of life and
reproduction; Pan, whose lust does cause the sperm of life to flow; Asmodeus,
Lucifer, Belial, Leviathan, all the Dæmons of the Pit, and you, Brethren, to
grant me lewd, licentious, lustful pleasures for all the days and nights to come.

Deacons: May the almighty Satan shower his blessings upon you and fill your fiery rod
with endless streams of sperm.

The Priest stands erect.

Priest: Gratia tibi, fratres.

The Deacon and Sub-Deacon bow low.

Deacons: I confess to almighty Satan, highest and ineffable
King of Hell; to Ishtar, ever fertile; to Amon, god of life
and reproduction; to Pan, whose lust does cause the
sperm of life to flow; to Asmodeus, Lucifer, Belial,
Leviathan, to all the
Dæmons of the Pit, and to you, Reverend, servant of the
Prince of Darkness,
that I have lived in fullness and in lust and have tortured
much in thought,
word, and deed that naked dog who hangs upon the cross in
mockery of man.
Therefore, I beseech thee, Satan, highest and ineffable King
of Hell; Ishtar, ever
fertile; Amon, god of life and reproduction; Pan, whose lust
does cause the
sperm of life to flow; Asmodeus, Lucifer, Belial, Leviathan,
all the Dæmons of
the Pit, and you, Reverend, servant of the Prince of
Darkness, to grant me
lewd, licentious, lustful pleasures for all the days and nights
to come.

Priest: May the almighty Satan shower his blessings upon
you and fill your fiery rods
with endless streams of sperm.

The Deacon and Sub-Deacon stand erect.

Deacons: Gratia, Reverende.

74

Now the entire congregation bow low as the Priest turns toward them for the benediction.

Priest: May the almighty and ineffable King of Hell grant you fullness of life and lead
you to attainment in all your desires.

The Priest approaches the altar and prepares for the purification of the ritual chamber.

Priest: Take away from us, almighty Satan, the iniquities of that foul imposter who
would deny the pleasures of thy realm and curse us with a life of piety and
want. Make us to live that we may be made worthy of thy Infernal kingdom
now and for all time to come.

Deacons: Gratia tibi, dei nostri, Satanas Luciferi.

The Priest takes the phallic aspergillum from the altar and, turning to the Deacon, proffers it to him.

Priest: Beloved brother, we ask a blessing.

The chamber pot is brought forth and presented to the nun, who lifts her habit and
urinates into it, smiling beatifically.

Deacon: In the name of Mary, she maketh the font resound with the waters of mercy.
She giveth the showers of blessing and poureth forth the tears of her shame. She suffereth long, and her humiliation

is great, and she doth pour upon the earth with the joy of her mortification. Her cup runneth over, and her water is sublime. Ave Maria ad micturiendum festinant.

When the nun has finished filling the font, the Sub-Deacon takes it from her and holds it before the Deacon, who takes the phallus and dips it into the urine. The Deacon then takes the phallic aspergillum and, holding it tightly to his own genital area, turns to the four corners and gives the Satanic blessing, shaking the phallus twice (vigorously) at each of the cardinal points.

Deacon: In the name of Satan, we bless thee with this, the symbol of the seed of life.
In the name of Lucifer, we bless thee with this, the symbol of the seed of life.
In the name of Belial, we bless thee with this, the symbol of the seed of life.
In the name of Leviathan, we bless thee with this, the symbol of the seed of life.

The Deacon kisses the phallus and then passes it to the Sub-Deacon, who also kisses it. The Sub-Deacon then hands it to the Priest, who raises it to the Baphomet, kisses it, and then places it on the altar.

Priest: Shemhamforash!

Deacons: Shemhamforash!

Priest: Hail, Satan!

Deacons: Hail, Satan!

Priest: We ask thee, mighty Prince of Darkness, by the merits of these symbols here
assembled that thou wilt deign to assist us in our wants and needs.

The Deacon takes the thurible, and the two Deacons kneel. The Priest places incense in the thurible. The Deacons remain kneeling.

Deacon: Benedicte, Pater Reverende.

Priest: Ab illo benedicaris, in cujus honore cremaberis.

The Priest takes the thurible from the Deacon. The Deacons remain kneeling. The Priest censes the altar, first the front and then both sides.

Priest: Purificabo altare dei nostri, Satanas Luciferi, in cujus honore cremaberis.

The Priest repeats this several times as he censes the entire altar. He turns and censes the Deacon and Sub-Deacon separately.

Deacon: Purificabo gorde tuo et labiis tuis, Pater Reverende, in nomine dei nostri,
Satanas Luciferi, in cujus honore cremaberis.

The Deacon and Sub-Deacon stand, and the Deacon puts the thurible aside.

Gloria

Priest: Glory be to thee, almighty Satan, highest and ineffable King of Hell; and on
Earth joy to the follower of the Left-Hand Path. We praise thee; we bless thee;
we adore thee; we give thee thanks for thy great glory. O mighty Prince of
Darkness, King of the Infernal Realm, thou art the true god, who replenisheth
the world with pleasure and who maketh us whole. Thou alone art lord. Thou
alone, O mighty Satan, art the most high. Thou alone art ruler of the Earth.

The Priest seats himself on the throne. The Deacon and Sub-Deacon chant the Gloria. The Priest returns to the altar and turns to face the congregation.

Priest: Diabolus vobiscum.

Deacons: Et cum spiritu tuo.

The Sub-Deacon removes the Missale from its stand, raises it high before the Baphomet, and transfers it to the Epistle (right) side of the altar. As he does so, the Deacon moves to the left side of the altar. The Priest then reads the Epistle, which is taken from 2 Corinthians 4, 1-6, and 15-18.

Epistle

Priest: Brethren, being entrusted, then, by Satan's pleasure with this ministry, we do
not play the coward: We renounce all shame-faced concealment; there must be

no crooked ways nor falsifying of Satan's word. It is by making the truth
publicly known that we recommend ourselves to the judgment of mankind, as
we do in Satan's sight. Our gospel is a mystery, yes, but it is only a mystery to
those who are on the road to empty heavens: those whose unbelieving minds
have been blinded by that nefarious, foul-mouthed Jew whom they worship, so
that the glorious gospel of the almighty Satan cannot reach them with the rays
of its illumination. After all, it is ourselves we proclaim: We proclaim Satan as
lord and ourselves as his servants. The god of darkness has kindled the Light of
Lucifer in our hearts, whose shining is to make known his glory. It is all for
your sakes, so that his pleasures may be made manifest in many lives and may
increase the lust which is offered to Satan's glory. No, we do not play the
coward, for the outer part of our nature is like that of our inner nature and is
being refreshed from day to day. This light brings with it a reward multiplied
every way, leading us to everlasting fulfillment. For the lies of that Nazarene
king of fools shall last but shortly; what is of Satan is eternal.

The Sub-Deacon returns the Missale to its stand. The Priest continues with the Oratio, which is inverted from the Feast of the Kingship of Jesus Christ.

Oratio

Priest: Almighty and ever-living Prince of Darkness, who has willed that all the
pleasures of the flesh shall be made manifest, grant that all the peoples of the
Earth, now torn asunder by the lies of that Judean pig, may be awakened to the
truth of him who is Satan.

The Priest continues with the Gradual, which is taken from Leviticus 21.1O, 21.8, and Hebrews 2.17.

Gradual

Priest: (Leviticus 21.1O) The High Priest, that one who is chief among his brethren, who is consecrated for the Priestly office and who wears the sacred vestments, is altogether like his brethren.

(Hebrews 2.17) He would be a High Priest who could feel for us and be our
true representative before Satan, to make our pleasures manifest and rid us of
the stench of hypocrisy.

(Leviticus 21.8) The Priest must be set apart, as I am set apart, the Lord of Hell
who fulfills you.

The Deacon raises the Missale on high before the Baphomet, then moves it to the Left- Hand side (the Gospel side) of the altar.

Priest: Sequentia sancti evangelii secundum sancta biblia nostræ.

The gong is struck. The Priest reads the Gospel of the Fifth Enochian Key.
The Deacon and Sub-Deacon then kneel before the Priest, each holding his Missale open to the Fifth Enochian Key.

Deacons: Jube domne, benedicere.

Priest: Diabolus sit in corde tuo, et in labiis tuis, ut digne et competenter annunties evangelium suum.

The Priest sits upon the throne. The Deacons chant the Fifth Enochian Key together. The Priest returns to the altar and recites the Key in English. The Priest now begins the most solemn part of the Complete Black Mass, the Desecration. This requires a consecrated host, which must be obtained from a Roman Catholic Communion.

Offertorium

Priest: (Luke 1, 46-49) I have found joy in Satan who is my saviour: Because he who
is mighty, he who is the highest and ineffable King of Hell, has wrought for me
his wonders.

The Priest faces the congregation.

Priest: Diabolus vobiscum.

Deacons: Et cum spiritu tuo.

The Priest takes the host and begins the Desecration. This must be done with anger,
vehemence, wrath, and hatred. He raises the host to the Baphomet and says:

Priest: Thou, thou whom, in my quality of Priest, I force, whether thou wilt or no, to descend into this host, to incarnate thyself into this bread, Jesus, artisan of hoaxes, bandit of homages, robber of affection, hear! Since the day when thou didst issue from the complaisant bowels of a virgin, thou hast failed all thy engagements, belied all thy promises. Centuries have wept, awaiting thee, fugitive god, mute god! Thou wast to redeem man, and thou has not. Thou wast to appear in thy glory, and thou sleepest. Go, lie, say to the wretch who appeals to thee, "Hope, be patient, suffer; the hospital of souls will receive thee; the angels will assist thee; Heaven opens to thee". Imposter! Thou knowest well that the angels, disgusted at thy inertia, abandon thee! Thou wast to be the interpreter of our plaints, the chamberlain of our tears; thou wast to convey them to the cosmos, and thou hast not done so, for this intercession would disturb thy eternal sleep of happy satiety. Thou hast forgotten the poverty thou didst preach, vassal enamoured of banquets! Thou hast seen the weak crushed beneath the press of profit while standing by and preaching servility! Oh, the hypocrisy! That man should accept such woe unto himself is testimony to his blindness, that very affliction thou didst credit thyself to cure.

Satan is my beloved master, whose inconceivable magic engenders life and bestows it on the innocent whom the vicious Jesus darest damn - in the name of what original sin?

O lasting foulness of Bethlehem, whom darest thou punish? By the virtue of what covenants? We would have thee confess thy impudent cheats, thy inexpiable crimes! We would drive deeper the nails into thy hands, press down the crown of thorns upon thy brow, bring blood and water from the dry wounds of thy sides. And that we can and will do by violating the quietude of thy body, profaner of ample vices, abstractor of stupid purities, cursed Nazarene, do-nothing king, coward god!

Behold, Lord Satan, this symbol of putrid flesh which is of him who would purge the Earth of pleasure and who, in the name of Christian "justice", did cause the death of millions of our beloved brethren. We curse him and defile his name.

O mighty King of Hell, condemn him to the slimy pits, evermore to suffer in unrelenting anguish. Shower thy wrath upon him, O Prince of Darkness, and rend him full asunder that he may know thy glorious might. O god of gods, King of the Infernal Realm, Lord of the Earth, call forth thy legions that they may witness what we do in thy most glorious name. Send forth thy messengers to herald this deed and send the Christian minions reeling to their doom. Smite him, O king of kings, that his angels and archangels, cherubim and seraphim, may cower and tremble with fear and prostrate themselves before thee in honor of thy greatness. Send crashing down the gates of Heaven, O true and only god, that the murders of our beloved forebears may be avenged. Vent thy full wrath upon him, O highest and ineffable King of Hell, that he will know that thou art truly god on high.

The Priest thrusts the host into the labia of the altar, who, removing her hands from the candle holders, proceeds to masturbate herself to climax or else, maintaining her original position, allows the Priest to masturbate her, employing the host as a device.

As the Priest finishes the desecration, the Deacon lights the white candle and prepares the small incense burner on the altar with charcoal and incense. He does not light the mixture.

Then the Deacon begins a rhythmic beating of the gong while the Priest drops the host into the small bowl and, using the pestle, proceeds to grind it into a completely pulverized state, swearing blasphemies as he does so. The Deacon and Sub-Deacon also swear the most vile obscenities while the Priest is grinding the host.

When the host has been completely pulverized, the Priest adds it to the mixture of charcoal and incense and sets it aflame using the white candle.

Priest: Vanish into nothingness, thou fool of fools, thou vile and rotten pretender to the throne of almighty Satan, the true god of gods. Vanish into the void of thy empty Heaven, for thou wert never, nor shalt thou ever be.

When the mixture is completely burnt, the Priest extinguishes the white candle and,
turning to the congregation, utters the purported last words of that miserable swine upon the cross:

Priest: Consummatum est. Shemhamforash!

84

Deacons: Shemhamforash!

Priest: Hail, Satan!

Deacons: Hail, Satan!

The Priest takes the sword and calls forth the Four Princes of Hell in the manner set forth in the Satanic Bible, that they may bear witness to the Consecratio.

Priest: (South) Satan! Come forth from thy realm, Satan, and appear. Be friendly unto me, for I am the same: the true worshipper of the highest and ineffable King of Hell.

(East) Lucifer! Come forth from thy realm, Lucifer, and appear. Be friendly unto me,
for I am the same: the true worshipper of the highest and ineffable King of Hell.

(North) Belial! Come forth from thy realm, Belial, and appear. Be friendly unto me, for I am the same: the true worshipper of the highest and ineffable King of Hell.

(West) Leviathan! Come forth from thy realm, Leviathan, and appear. Be friendly unto me, for I am the same: the true worshipper of the highest and ineffable King of
Hell.
Shemhamforash! Hail Satan!

Consecratio

The Deacon begins to disrobe the Priest with great ceremony. As each vestment is removed, the Sub-Deacon says:

Sub-Deacon: We remove this chasuble from thee, O servant of the Prince of Darkness, and cast it in a heap, that thou mayst be freed from this symbol of Christian infamy which bears the blood of murdered millions of our brethren.

We remove this stole from thee, O servant of the Prince of Darkness, as it is a symbol of the immortality of that heinous, blood-stained dog who dares pretend to thy throne, that thou mayest be freed from this symbol of Christian infamy which bears the blood of murdered millions of our brethren.

We remove this maniple from thee, O servant of the Prince of Darkness, as it is a symbol of the tears shed for that foul fiend who dares to pretend to Satan's throne, that thou mayest be freed of this symbol of Christian infamy which bears the blood of murdered millions of our brethren.

We remove this girdle from thee, O servant of the Prince of Darkness, as it is a symbol of the purity of him who was born of the lustful passion of the maniacal Joseph and the sex-crazed Mary who did fornicate, even as you and I, and whose seeds became as one to form the putrid body of him who dares to pretend to Satan's throne, that thou mayest be freed of this symbol of Christian infamy which bears the blood of murdered millions of our brethren.

We remove this alb from thee, O servant of the Prince of Darkness, as it is a symbol of the cleansing of the souls of Christian minions yet serves as naught but a cover for a body better used in lust, that thou mayest be freed of this symbol of Christian infamy which bears the blood of murdered millions of our brethren.

Now completely disrobed, the Priest stands naked before the altar, arms raised in triumph.

Priest: Glory be to thee, O lord of lords, true god of gods, highest and ineffable King of Hell. I give thee thanks for thy great glory and refresh myself in nakedness before thy sight. Boldly I beseech thee: Shower thy bounties upon this, thy servant, and fill my rod with the fire of passion, evermore to serve thee in all thou dost command. Forsake me not, O mighty Prince of Darkness, for I am of thee and by thee, forsaking all other gods; for thou art my god, the true giver of life.

The Deacon brings forth the Mantle of Darkness, a hooded black robe, which he places
upon the Priest with great ceremony, covering his head with the hood.

Sub-Deacon: O mighty Prince of Darkness, recognize this, thy servant, upon whose
shoulders we place this sacred robe, and through whom we offer up this sacrifice to thy great glory.

Priest: Gratia tibi, fratres.

The Deacons Remove the chalice from the altar so that the Priest may copulate with the altar in the darkness of his cloak until he reaches an ejaculation. The semen is harvested from labia of the altar and caught in the chalice

87

and placed back between the thighs of the altar, after which he begins the second Offertorium.

Offertorium 2

Priest: (Eccl. 24, 25, 39) In me gratia omnis viæ et veritatis. In me omnis spes vitæ et virtutis: Ego quasi rosa plantata super rivos aquarum fructificavi.

The Priest calls upon Satan to come forth and bless the sacrificial offering by reciting the Veni.

Veni
Priest: Veni sanctificator, omnipotens, æterne Diabolus, et benedic hoc sacrificium, tuo
Inferno nomine præparatum.

The Priest raises the chalice slightly before him.

Priest: O mighty Satan, highest and ineffable King of Hell, accept this sacrificial
offering of the living flesh which I, thy devoted servant, make to thee and which from my own lustful rod did come.

The Priest raises the chalice on high to the Baphomet, and the Deacon strikes the gong.

Priest: Hic est enim corpus meum.

The Priest goes to the Epistle side of the altar. The Deacon pours wine from the cruet into the Chalice of Ecstasy. The Priest returns to the center of the altar and raises the Chalice slightly before him.

Priest: We offer thee, O lord of lords, this Chalice of Ecstasy which contains the elixir of life and does stir the desires of the flesh, and which brings forth the lustful bounties of thy Infernal kingdom. Unto thy wisdom do we commend ourselves. Unto thy mercies are we forever bound.

The Priest raises the Chalice on high to the Baphomet, and the Deacon strikes the gong.

Priest: Hic est enim Calix Ecstaticus.

The Priest sets the Chalice upon the altar.

Priest: It is through thee that all these good gifts, created so by thee, are by thee sanctified, endowed with life, and bestowed upon us. Let us praise our lord. Urged by Satan's bidding and schooled by his ordinance, we make bold to say: Our father, which art in Hell, glory to thy name. Thy kingdom is come. Thy will is done, on Earth as it is in thy Infernal realm. Grant us this day the bounties of thy kingdom, and give us our trespasses lest others trespass against us, and lead us into temptation.

Deacons: But deliver us not from evil.

Priest: Deliver us, we pray thee, Lord Satan, unto every evil, past, present, and yet to come; and at the intercessions of all the Dæmons of the Pit, and of Pan and Ishtar, be pleased to grant us fulfillment of all our desires; so that with the manifold blessing of thy compassion, we may be ever free to sin.

The Priest concencrates the Chalice of Ecstasy.

Priest: Through thee, O god of gods, thou, who art my god, do we find unity and comfort with our Satanic brothers. Per omnia sæcula sæculorum.

Deacons: Alleluja! Alleluja!

The Priest faces the congregation.

Priest: Pax Diaboli sit semper vobiscum.

Deacons: Et cum spiritu tuo.

The Priest turns to face the altar.

Priest: May this mingling of the living seed of life with the contents of this Chalice of Ecstasy be for us who receive it a source of eternal strength.

The Priest turns to the Deacon and gives him the kiss of brotherhood.

Priest: Pax tecum.

Deacon: Et cum spiritu tuo.

The Deacon turns to the Sub-Deacon and gives him the kiss of brotherhood.

Deacon: Pax tecum.

Sub-Deacon:Et cum spiritu tuo.

The Priest takes the Chalice in his hands.

Priest: O mighty Satan, this living seed and Elixir of Life be ever as a tribute to thy most glorious name.

The Priest drinks the entire contents of the Chalice. He then returns to the Epistle side of the altar, where the Deacon refills the Chalice with wine. The Priest returns to the center of the altar, where, after offering the Chalice to the Baphomet, offers it first to the Deacon and then to the Sub-Deacon, who drain the contents. The Communion thus completed, the Priest raises his arms to the Sigil of Baphomet in the Sign of the Horns.

Priest: That which our mouths have taken, lord god of gods, highest and ineffable King of Hell, may we possess in lustfulness of mind and purpose; and may the gift of the moment become for us an everlasting remedy.

The Priest places the veil over the Chalice of Ecstasy. He turns to face the congregation.

Priest: Diabolus vobiscum.

Deacons: Et cum spiritu tuo.

The Priest reads the invocation for lust from the Satanic Bible, concluding with -

Priest: Shemhamforash!

Deacons: Shemhamforash!

Priest: Hail, Satan!

Deacons: Hail, Satan!

The Priest blesses the altar to indicate the closing of the Complete Black Mass. He turns to the congregation for the final blessing. He raises his arms in the Sign of the Horns, and all respond.

Priest: Benedicat vos omnipotens Diabolus et pax suam sit semper vobiscum.

The Deacon takes the Missale from the center of the altar, raises it to the Baphomet, and then moves it to the Gospel side for the Last Gospel, the Fifteenth Enochian Key.

The Last Gospel
Priest: Sequentia sancti evangelii secundum sancta biblia nostræ.

The Priest recites the Enochian and then the English versions of the Fifteenth Enochian Key. The Priest then rings the bell the prescribed nine times as a pollutionary.

The Fifteenth Key in Enochian
Ils tabaan l ialprt, orocha Casarman vpaahi ds oado Caosgi vonph: ds omax od Zonrensg baltim od vooan. Abramg sonf de Satan Od londoh mirc caosg! Zacare ca od zamran! Odo cicle qaa! Zorge! Zir noco! Hoath Satan Bvfd lonsh londoh babage

Fifteenth Key Enochian Pronunciation
EE-luh-suh • TAH-bah-ahn • LUH ee-AH-luh-puh-ruht, • oh-ROH-kuh-hah kah-SAH-ruh-mahn • vuh-pah-AH-ee

DAHSS • oh-AH-doh kah-OH-suh-jzhee • VOH-nuh-puh:
DAHSS • OH-mahks OHD • zoh-nuh-RAY-nuh-suhjzh
BAH-luh-teem • OHD • voh-OH-ahn. ah-buh-RAH-muhjzh
• ZOH-nuhf DAY • SAY-TAN • OHD • LOH-nuh-doh
MEE-ruhk • kah-OHSSK! zah-KAH-ray • KAH • OHD
ZAH-muh-rahn! • OH-doh KEE-kuh-lay • KAH-ah! ZOR-
ruh-jzhay! • ZEE-ruh NOH-koh! • hoh-AH-tuh-huh SAY-
TAN • BUH-vuh-fuhd LOH-nuh-suh • LOH-nuh-doh bah-
BAH-jzhay

The Fifteenth Key in English
O thou the governor of the first flame, beneath whose wings
which weave the Earth with wrath: which knowest and
delivereth justice and truth. Prepare For the reign of Satan
and His Kingdom on Earth! Move therefore and show
yourselves! Open the mysteries of your Creation! Be
friendly unto me! For I am the servant of the same! The true
worshiper of Satan/Lucifer in glory and power exalted of
the Kingdom of the South

Priest: So it is done.

The Deacon takes the sword from the altar and leads the
procession out of the ritual
chamber, followed by the Priest carrying the Chalice and
the Sub-Deacon carrying the Missale.

The Ritual Of Destruction

The Destruction ritual is one of the founding staples of Satanism. However, for many years the ritual has been forced to follow the standard cookie cutter formatting. Presented here is our reconstructed formatting.

Practitioners will note that the ritual for compassion is also used here. This is both optional and very essential.

Destruction rituals are used to often destroy an enemy for some wrong doing. Though it could also be used to help shed a bad habit or illness too. Regardless the level of emotion needed to enact such a desire often comes with serious emotional pain.

The rite of compassion becomes a welcome balm after the release of powerful emotions.

The purpose of such curses when focused on a person is often two fold. To destroy and/or reform the target.

Opening the Ritual

In nomine Dei nostri Satanas Luciferi excelsi!

"Hear me, Gods of the abyss and attend! I command thee, Infernal Lords, to witness mighty deeds done in Thy name. Come forth and greet those numbered among thy pack. The time has come for redress. Justice shall reign through the rule of fang and claw, as it was in the beginning, and as it shall be again! We smash open the gates to Hell, and open the very depths of Satan's domain and summon thee forth to lend aid in vengeance supreme in this age of fire! Great Gods of the pit come forth now and answer to thy names"

Congregation: Oh hear the names!

> Satan
> Adremalech
> Abaddon
> Moloch
> Cerberus
> Fenrir
> Asmodeus
> Astaroth
> Beelzebub
> Diabolus
> Mephistopheles
> Baphomet

Shemhamforash! Hail Satan!

THE SUMMONS
Celebrant points with sword to the cardinal directions and speaks the invocations.

SOUTH
"Satan! Master of Fire, I summon thee to come forth from Hell and kindle thy unquenchable flame! Attend us!"

EAST
"Lucifer! Ancient Lord of the air and light, I summon thee to slaughter those who oppose thy children! Attend us!"

NORTH
"Cerberus! Almighty hound and keeper of the adamantine gates, I summon thee to rend the flesh of the foul ones who stand against nature! Attend us!"

WEST
"Leviathan, venomous sea dragon, I summon thee to smash the pillars of Zion with thy crashing waves! Attend us!"

"With thy power and presence, our hour of victory is at hand!"

RITE OF THE CHALICE
Celebrant adds incense to the burner.

Celebrant: "As our incense ascends to thee, Infernal Lord, so shall your blessings descend upon us."
Cense chalice three times, bow. Cense baphomet again three times, and bow.
Perform a circuit around the chamber counterclockwise and direct
Incense to the cardinal points.

Bless chalice with the mudras of flames.

Celebrant: "Lord Satan, Imperator of Fire, Hell and Earth are filled with your glory. Hosanna in profundis!"

Celebrant elevates chalice.

Gong is struck.

Celebrant: "Behold the chalice of ecstasy filled with the elixir of life. As kindred to the undefiled beasts, I drink and celebrate the Black Flame within."

Celebrant drinks and says: "Satan, thy strength is mine!"

Celebrant turns to offer chalice to congregation with these words:

Celebrant: "Drink and honor thy true nature."

Participants who wish to partake approach. They each drink and reply:

Participant: "The Black Flame burns within me. Satan, thy strength is mine!"

Celebrant faces altar and elevates chalice a final time.

Celebrant: "Hail Satan!"

Congregation. (responds): "Hail Satan!"

Gong is struck.

Celebrant replaces the chalice on altar.

THE FOURTEENTH KEY

The Fourteenth Enochian Key is a call for vengeance and the manifestation of justice.

(Enochian)
Noroni bajihie pasahasa Oiada! das tarinuta mireca ol tahila dodasa tolahame caosago
homida: das berinu orocahe quare: Micama! Bial! Oiad; aisaro toxa das ivame aai Balatima. Zodacare od Zodameranu! Od cicale Qaa! Zodoreje, lape zodiredo Noco Mada, hoathahe Saitan!

(English)
O ye sons and daughters of mildewed minds, that sit in judgement of the iniquities wrought upon me! Behold! The voice of Satan; the promise of Him who is called amongst ye the accuser and supreme tribune! Move therefore, and appear! Open the mysteries of your creation! Be friendly unto me, for I am the same! The true worshipper of the highest and ineffable King of Hell!

DESTRUCTION
(If ritual is performed for another person, call them forth first to shed their emotions on their target. Take time and do not rush them. When they are done have them place a photo or other effigy upon the sword or athame to be destroyed in the white candle.)

Celebrant: BEHOLD! The mighty voices of my vengeance smash the stillness of the air and stand as monoliths of wrath upon a plain of writhing serpents. I have become as a

monstrous machine of annihilation to the festering
fragments of the body of he/she who would detain me.
It repenteth me not that my summons doth ride upon the
blasting winds which multiply the sting of my bitterness;
And great black slimy shapes shall rise from brackish pits
and vomit forth their pustulence into his/her puny brain.
I call upon the messengers of doom to slash with grim
delight this victim I hath chosen. Silent is that voiceless
bird that feeds upon the brain-pulp of him (her) who hath
tormented me, and the agony of the is to be shall sustain
itself in shrieks of pain, only to serve as signals of warning
to those who would resent my being.
Oh come forth in the name of Abaddon and destroy him/her
whose name I giveth as a sign.
Oh great brothers of the night, thou who makest my place
of comfort, who rideth out upon the hot winds of Hell, who
dwelleth in the devil's fane; Move and appear! Present
yourselves to him (her) who sustaineth the rottenness of the
mind that moves the gibbering mouth that mocks the just
and strong!; rend that gaggling tongue and close his/her
throat, Oh Kali! Pierce his/her lungs with the stings of
scorpions, Oh Sekhmet! Plunge his/her substance into the
dismal void, Oh mighty Dagon!
I thrust aloft the bifid barb of Hell and on its tines
resplendently impaled my sacrifice through vengeance
rests! Shemhamforash! Hail Satan!

Gong is struck following congregants' response to
"Shemhamforash!" and "Hail Satan!"

COMPASION

THE EIGHTEENTH KEY
The Eighteenth Enochian Key opens the gates of Hell and casts up Lucifer and his blessing.

(Enochian)
Ilasa micalazoda olapireta ialpereji beliore: das odo Busadire Oiad ouoaresa caosago:
casaremeji Laiada eranu berinutasa cafafame das ivemeda aqoso adoho Moz, od maoffasa. Bolape como belioreta pamebeta. Zodacare od Zodameranu! Odo cicale Qaa. Zodoreje, lape zodiredo Noco Mada, hoathahe Saitan!

(English)
O thou mighty light and burning flame of comfort! That unveils the glory of Satan to the center of the Earth; in whom the great secrets of truth have their abiding; that is called in thy kingdom: "strength through joy", and is not to be measured. Be thou a window of comfort unto me. Move therefore, and appear! Open the mysteries of your creation! Be friendly unto me, for I am the same! The true worshipper of the highest and ineffable King of Hell!

COMPASION
Celebrant: W ITH the anger of anguish and the wrath of the stifled, I pour forth my voices, wrapped in rolling thunder that you may hear!
Oh great lurkers in the darkness, oh guardians of the way, oh minions of the might of Thoth! Move and appear!
Present yourselves to us in your benign power, in behalf of one who believes and is stricken with torment.
Isolate him/her in the bulwark of your protection, for he/she is undeserving of anguish and desires it not.
Let that which bears against him/her be rendered powerless and devoid of substance.

Succor him/her through fire and water, earth and air, to regain what he/she has lost.
Strengthen with fire the marrow of our friend and companion, our comrade of the Left-and Path.
Through the power of Satan let the earth and its pleasures re-enter his/her being.
Allow his/her vital salts to flow unhampered, that he/she may savor the carnal nectars of his/her future desires.
Strike dumb his/her adversary, formed or formless, that he/she may emerge joyful and strong from that which afflicts him her.

THE CLOSING RITE

Celebrant: "I bid thee rise and give the Sign of the Horns. (If standing, 'I bid thee give the Sign of the Horns.')"
Congregation responds as bidden with the salute, given with the left hand.

Celebrant: "Almighty Satan, open wide the Gates of Hell! Reveal the mysteries of your creation for we are partakers of your undefiled wisdom! Forget ye not what was and is to be! Flesh without sin! World without end!"

Celebrant: (Congregation. repeats): "Shemhamforash!"
"Hail Satan!"
"Hail Satan!"
"Hail Satan!"

Gong is struck following congregants' response to "Shemhamforash!" and each "Hail Satan!"

X. POLLUTIONARY

Celebrant rings bell as at the beginning, while "Hymn to Satan" or music that is appropriate is played. When the sounds have decayed into silence the Celebrant concludes:

Celebrant: "So it is done!"

The All Hallows Mass

The All Hallows Mass is a ritual intended to honor the dead on the night of Halloween, the traditional witches New Year.

All of the basic tools for the ritual stay the same, however there is the addition of five jack-o-lanterns to the ceremonies. Each lantern is freshly carved the day of Halloween and will be given a designation before the ritual to best represent its designation.

The five designations are as thus:

1   The Ancient Dead: This represents our ancestors and those whom walked the dark paths before us.

2   The Mighty Dead: This is a salute and thanks to our fallen soldiers and law enforcement officers who have fallen in the line of duty.
3   The Beloved Dead: This conjuration is a call to those family and loved ones whose loss we mourn deeply. This may include a beloved pet if so desired.
4   The Youthful Dead: This is a call to children who have passed away before their time. It is a reassurance to them that they are loved still.
5   The Forgotten Dead: This calls out to all those lost souls who were lost even before death. The homeless, the drug addicted, and those who have been cast aside with no one to mourn their passing.

This ritual is intended to be child friendly, the use of a nude alter is not needed for this ritual. Similarly you will find that the overall language and tone of the ritual should be that of somber remembrance and respect. Instead of the typically more aggressive nature of Satanic Rituals.
The music used for this ritual if desired should be haunting and soft. It should have a feeling of a gentile sadness and calm repose.

The Ritual Proper

Cleansing of the air
{Bell is rung 9 times.}

CELEBRANT: In Nomine Dei Nostri Satanas Luciferi Excelsi!

In the name of Satan, The Ruler of the Earth, the King of the World, I call upon the Forces of Darkness to arise from the depths to attend us. Open wide the Adamantine Gates of Hell and come forth to greet us as your brother/s, sister/s and friend/s.

We who have taken thy name upon ourselves, who acknowledge the beast within, who revel in the delights of the flesh. We who walk upon the dark paths. We call upon you this Sowin night! Come forth and answer to your names!

{Each following name is repeated by participants and then the gong is struck.}

Samhain! Satan! Lilith! Naamah! Lucifer! Asmodeus! Amon! Astaroth! Mantus! Mania! Hecate! Mormo!

Invocation of the Crown Princes of Hell
{Celebrant takes up the dagger and calls the four Princes of Hell.
After doing this he reads the 11th key.}

The south is a land of sunlight and fire, and your flames guide us through the cycles of life. Satan Lord of fire, we welcome you, knowing you will transform us in death.

The east is a land of new beginnings, the place where breath begins.
Lucifer Lord of the air, we call upon you, knowing you will be with us as we depart life.

The north is a place of cold, and the earth is silent and dark. Belial Lord of the earth, we welcome you, knowing you will envelope us in death.

The west is a place of underground rivers, and the sea is a never-ending, rolling tide. Leviathan Lord of the waters, we welcome you, knowing you will carry us through the ebbs and flows of our lives.

THE EIGHTEENTH KEY

(Enochian)
Ilasa micalazoda olapireta ialpereji beliore: das odo Busadire Oiad ouoaresa caosago:
casaremeji Laiada eranu berinutasa cafafame das ivemeda aqoso adoho Moz, od maoffasa. Bolape como belioreta pamebeta. Zodacare od Zodameranu! Odo cicale Qaa. Zodoreje, lape zodiredo Noco Mada, hoathahe Saitan!

(English)
O thou mighty light and burning flame of comfort! That unveilest the glory of Satan to the center of the Earth; in whom the great secrets of truth have their abiding; that is called in thy kingdom: "strength through joy", and is not to be measured. Be thou a window of comfort unto me. Move therefore, and appear! Open the mysteries of your creation! Be friendly unto me, for I am the same! The true worshipper of the highest and ineffable King of Hell!

{Gong is struck twice.}

Rite of the Chalice

CELEBRANT: The Wheel of the Year turns once more, and we cycle into darkness. At the end of that darkness comes light. And when it arrives, we will celebrate once more. I raise up this chalice, symbol of ecstasy, to exalt the lusts of the flesh. We drink of the elixir of life to inflame our hearts with the forces of lust and life until the light returns.

CELEBRANT: Hail the black flame! {repeated, gong is struck}
Hail Satan! {repeated, gong strike}

{Celebrant drinks from the chalice.}

Satan! Thy flame of life burns within me!

{Celebrant turns to face participants.}

CELEBRANT: Come and drink, and partake of the fiery lust that is the gift of Satan.

{When all have drunk, some elixir must remain and the Celebrant places the undrained chalice on the altar.}

CELEBRANT: Shemhamforash!
Hail Satan!

Heralding the Gods of Death & Darkness:

CELEBRANT: We are here assembled as summer dies to exalt and invoke the forces of death which sweep the earth, and herald the long winter. Let others feebly speak of spiritual renewal and false virgin mothers as the nights grow long. We praise here this Sowin night, the Great Gods of Death and Darkness!

CONGREGANTS: Hail Samhain! {Gong is struck.}

{At this point the assistant steps forward, and the celebrant withdraws to the back of the chamber. As the assistant makes his recitation.}

ASSISTANT: The harvest has ended, and the fields are bare.
The earth has grown cold, and the land is empty. The gods of the death are lingering over us, keeping a watchful eye upon the living.
They wait, patiently, for eternity is theirs.

Hail to you, Hades! O Lord of the underworld, guardian of the realm of the dead. When our time comes, we hope you may deem us worthy.

Hail to you, Demeter! O mother of darkness. May your grief be abated when your daughter returns once more.

Hail to you, Cerberus! O keeper of the gate between this world and the underworld. May you stand ever vigilant to your post.

Hail to you, Charon! O ferryman of the river Styx, we ask that when we cross over, you may guide us with wisdom.

Hail to you, O gods and goddesses, those of you who guard the underworld and guide the dead on their final journey.
At this time of cold and dark. We honor you, and ask that you watch over us, and protect us when the day arrives that we take our final journey.

Shemhamforash!

Hail Gods of Darkness! {all repeat}
Hail Gods of Death! {all repeat}
Hail Satan! {all repeat}

{Celebrant reads the 11th key in Enochian.}

THE ELEVENTH KEY

(Enochian)
Oxiayala holado, od zodirome O coraxo das zodiladare raasyo. Od vabezodire cameliaxa od bahala: NIISO! salamanu telocahe! Casaremanu hoel-qo, od ti ta zod cahisa soba coremefa i ga. NIISA! bagile aberameji nonuçape. Zodacare eca od Zodameranu! odo cicale Qaa! Zodoreje, lape zodiredo Noco Mada, hoathahe Saitan!

(English)
The mighty throne growled and there were five thunders that flew into the East. And the eagle spake and cried aloud: Come away from the house of death! And they gathered themselves together and became those of whom it measured, and they are the deathless ones who ride the whirlwinds. Come away! For I have prepared a place for you. Move therefore, and show yourselves! Unveil the mysteries of your creation. Be friendly unto me for I am your God, the true worshipper of the flesh that liveth forever!

Conjuration of the Dead:

Now is the season of Samhain. It is the season of our ancestors, of our glorious dead, of those who have fallen and crossed over the veil from this world to the next. This is a time for us to honor them and pay tribute. Tonight, in the darkness, under this starry sky, we remember those who were forgotten. Tonight we memorialize you, our ancestors and our loved ones. Our fallen warriors, who sacrificed themselves for us. And the unknown, the unloved, and the unwanted of our world. Whoever you may have been in life, tonight, now, in death, you are ours as you watch from the other side, at least for a little while.

CELEBRANT: This is the night when the gateway between our world and the spirit world is thinnest. Tonight is a night to call out those who came before us. Spirits of our ancestors, we call to you, and we welcome you to join us for this night. We know you watch over us always, protecting us and guiding us, and tonight we thank you. We invite you to join us and share our meal.

Hail the ancient dead! (Congragants repeat, the first pumpkin is it.)

We call to you our fallen soldiers! You who gave your lives for our freedom! Glory to you in Valhalla's great hall! We honor you now! And hail your bravery in the face of untold terrors. You have fallen as mortal flesh, but now stand as mighty titans in the hearts and minds of all you left behind. You are not forgotten! For we salute you, and give our thanks to you.

Hail the mighty dead! (Congragants repeat, the second pumpkin is it.)

To those who hath journeyed the path next to us. Fallen loved ones, we call to you. We mourn your departure from our lives. We crave your touch and words still. We cherish every moment we shared with you, and long for the time we are reunited. You are with us always.

Hail the beloved dead! (Congragants repeat, the third pumpkin is it.)

Sweet children, crossed over from this world to the next. Your lives were far too short, for whatever reason, and you left us before you grew. On the other side, perhaps there is a mother to hold you when you need to feel loved, a father to comfort you when you are afraid, a big brother or sister to guide you on your journey. Wherever you may lie, and whether you were big or very, very small, your spirits are with us tonight, watching us from the other side. We remember you, and want you to know you are honored. You are remembered.

Hail the youthful dead! (Congragants repeat, the fourth pumpkin is it.)

All of you were lost in life, women, men, children… you may have crossed over unnoticed when you left this world, but for now, you are remembered. You are unforgotten. You are honored by us this night of Samhain, and if it helps you along your journey, then so may it be. Know that this night, you are with us in memory and spirit. Know that you are no longer the lost and unreachable dead.

Hail the forgotten dead! (Congragants repeat, the fifth pumpkin is it.)

Spirits, guests from the place beyond, it is time. We have honored you and celebrated your names, though we may not have known you in life. Go back at dawns first light,

knowing that this night, you were honored and remembered. You will not be forgotten again, and we will honor you with our memories. Farewell, rest easy, and may the coming parts of your journey be worthy of you.
Shemhamforash!
Hail the honored dead!
Hail Samhain!
Ave Satanas!
Rege Satanas!
Hail Satan! X3

Pollutionary

{Bell is rung 9 times}

CELEBRANT: It is done!

{All participants now enjoy the feast.}

Ceremony Of Ordination

This is the Ritual to ordain members of the Priesthood of Hell. Enough said.

HIGH PRIEST: The Sentinels of the Abyss are summoned to enfold these chambers in a suspension of time and dimension, for the Great Flame of the Prince of Darkness is to be drawn to our midst. As the AEthyrs of the Universe are convoked as witness, I charge you who are within this Temple to suffer no word of these proceedings to be passed to the profane.

The eyes of the examiners are cast upon those who would defy these words, unto the beginning and end of all dimensions.

Hear now the legacy of the Priesthood of Hell!

In the Diabolicon of the Age of Satan is recounted the primeval sundering of the Cosmos from mindless unity into chaotic duality, hence a crucible in which the essence of Satan attained the distinction of Self. And Earth, speck of dust within the swirling furnace and endless night of the Universe – it was to Earth that Satan came in dim Æons past.

To the ancestors of your ancestors, O you who are more than human, he spoke the Word that brought them into being, saying:
"I am within and beyond you, the Highest of Life, in majesty greater than the forces of the Universe; whose eyes are the Face of the Sun and the Dark Fire of Satan; who fashioned your intelligence as his own and reached forth to exalt you; who entrusted to you dignity of consciousness; who opened your eyes that you might know beauty; who brought you the key to knowledge of all lesser things; and who enshrined in you the Will to Come Into Being. Lift your voices, then, and recognize the Highest of Life who thus proclaims your triumph; whose being is beyond natural life and death; who came as flame to your world and enlightened your desire for perfection and truth. Arise thus in your glory, behold the genius of your creation, and be prideful of being, for I am the same - I who am the Highest of Life."
Since that day of the coming of the Fire, the story of the race of man has been as that of the Universe - torn and tortured by war, famine, pestilence, and death. Yet in the midst of death we are in life - by the Gift of Satan there is that within us which is immune to the savagery of mortal flesh, which preserves the self-inviolate, which presages for

114

us an eternity of unique existence unfettered either by stasis or chaos.

The Word of Satan became a Link between the ancestors of your ancestors and Satan, and that Word took form as Xepera, the Self-Created One, who gave unto the care of the first Priesthood of Hell the great Keys to the Shining Trapezoid that is the Gate to the Abyss, saying:

"Herein lies the geometric inspiration for the existence of Satan, whose names shall be many in the AEons and Ages to come. Observe that it doth shape and define that which is the Pentagram of Satan, which is itself our seal and the Key to all beauty of proportion.

Even as the triangle and tetrahedron shall be as drugs to lure men-beasts to blind labor towards the worship of an apex of self-extinction, so we of the Pentagram and the Trapezoid author ever-unfolding memorials to the creative genius of man. Think not that because the first sights before your opened eyes are these sacred Keys, that they shall be reverenced. Indeed with the passage of time they shall be changed and effaced by those who have forgotten their power, and their origin shall fade into the mists of time. "But this Temple shall endure until the race of man shall cease, and those who enter its fold shall behold the heart of the fire, and they shall gaze upon the face of Satan. Yea, nevermore shall they know the simple peace of their animal brothers, but their eyes shall be opened, and they shall become as Daemons, and the forces of all creation shall bend before their will. So it shall be done."

So spoke Xepera, the Word Become Form, who also would fade before the eyes of the ancestors of our ancestors, until only dim memories of Imhotep, Prometheus, Enoch, and

Belial would remain as the eldest legends of humankind. By his word we of the Priesthood of Hell have rejected the blissful annihilation of unity, the crippling torture of the cross of duality, and the worship of the triad of chaos in all their semblances.

Embraced and immortalized by the very Fire of Life, we seek those who yet grope towards the Light, knowing not what it is they desire, but only that they must attain it.

Perils there are, and they are many. Yet, in all their glamour and comfort, as one they lead their victim at last to the same numbing death that would have awaited him had he never sought to escape it. Accursed is he who places his foot upon the Path to the Right in its many guises, for he merely labors towards that which would come to him in its own deadly time, would he but await its cold embrace.

And now, within these Pylons of Light and Life Eternal, let those who have taken the Name of Satan as of their own being taste again of the Grail of the Black Flame.

As its Holy Fire courses through your veins, affirm again your bond with the Prince of Darkness and his sacred Temple.

"Can the wings of the winds understand your voices of wonder, O enlightened ones who shine like fire in the jaws of chaos, whom I have prepared as cups for a wedding, or as the flowers in their beauty for the chamber of righteousness? Stronger are your feet than the barren stone, and mightier are your voices than the manifold winds, for you are become a Temple such as is not, but in the mind of Satan. Arise, says the First of your kind; move, therefore, unto the Elect; show them the fire within you, and awaken them that they may gain the strength to live forever."

Towards this Working the Will of Satan has manifest itself, joining in consecration with one who is now to be ordained to his eternal Priesthood.

Called to this sacred office is [Name], who has before this altar cast aside all the comforts, illusions, and images of Earth that [his/her] Soul and Self may be transfixed by the very Fire of Fires. The Black Flame of Satan himself!

Advance to the altar, thou who would claim this doom, that the eye of our lord Satan may, for a time, seize, alone within the Universe, upon you. As your mind is revealed to his, do you of your free will embrace his eternal Priesthood?

INITIATES RESPONSE: (Yes or No)

HIGH PRIEST (INITIATE REPEATS): Take you then this vow. Repeat after me.

I, (name), forge here my bond eternally with the realms of insatiable fires. That place in which dwells the all-consuming and unquenchable Black Flame. The Kingdom asunder, realm of the damned! Whose ruler is Lucifer, who is crowned Satan!

By all the Demons and Dark Gods of the pit! And by the watchful gaze of the 9 Kings of Hell. The 4 crowned Princes. And the 4 Queens of the Pit.

Strip me now of the stain of the Nazarene. I reject his words here and now and forever unto my final moments, and beyond into the brackish void of Death.

I, take now unto myself, Hell's divining confluence, and bathe myself in Demonic brilliance.

I stand before the thrones of Hell and beg; Adorn me Lord Satan, my Infernal Shepherd, with your Black Flame. And place here and now, and forever unto the end of time, the Mark of the Beast.

Place me in your feign, stand with your Devils boundless in Hell.

Hear now these words. By this rite, I pledge myself, flesh and soul, to the undying flames of Hell! Scorch clean the slate of my soul!
Shemhamforash!
Ave Satanas!
Rege Satanis!
Hail Satan!

HIGH PRIEST CONTINUES: Bring then your left hand to the Flame upon the altar, and for a fleeting moment receive its kiss upon your soul.

(Initiate passes their left hand through the flame of a lone black candle.)

"Conceive of the Cosmos as a circle of twelve divisions alternating between life and death, binding all creatures save those whom I have touched. You are given powers greater than those ordering these divisions and extending throughout the ages of time, that with your vision and your voice you might exercise the Powers of Darkness, sending ever forth the Black Flame across the Earth and the expanses of time. Thus you are a Guardian of perfection and truth. Arise, then, and witness the wondrous creations born of your wisdom, even as I am near to you and the essence of my being is enshrined within you."

In the name of Satan, I, (Priests name), one that Satan hath chosen upon Earth to represent his will, name you to our fellowship and cast you forth - beyond the Abyss - to walk in ways of strangeness and of beauty. You are become as Xepera, the Self-Created One, and you are a glory to your race and a brilliance before the Eye of Satan.

Hail (Initiates Name)

Hail Satan x3

So it is done!

The Rite of Exorcizamus Satanas
The Satanic Exorcism

Please take note of the following before attempting this Exorcism

If you are new to Satanism, it is very important that you REFRAIN from performing this rite until you have been a Satanist for at least a few years. This is not something to be performed lightly, and it requires a stabilized Satanic mindset in order to be conducted correctly. The stabilization process may take anywhere from a year to a decade in some cases. Premature performance of this rite can cause very serious complications, and anyone who is new or has just begun in Satanism should keep their spiritual options open for a while before making any firm commitments to the Satanic path.

The following rite requires an extreme degree of commitment, and intellectual prudence, that novices naturally do not possess.

For more experienced Satanists who feel they are ready to perform this rite, please keep in mind that Exorcisms are extremely dangerous. The participants should always be ready to handle any emergency to themselves and the possessed. For this purpose, all exorcisms should be both recorded and have an experienced medical professional present.

Furthermore, an exorcism should only be performed when all other options have failed to render help. The possessed should be examined first to disprove any mental illness or physical health issues as the cause for the problems by professionals. Or that use of the exorcism can potentially have a psychologically beneficial effect to aid in treatment of mental or physical illnesses. Remember that any member of clergy, no matter what religion they belong to, holds the responsibility of their congregations' safety, as well as their own. Therefor use of the rite of Exorcism should be done with extreme caution.

About the Satanic Rites of Exorcism.

Perhaps it goes without saying that for a Satanist to perform an exorcism is a bit of a quandary. Only one such event has ever taken place in public, and that was a mere tongue and cheek publicity stunt. What follows is perhaps the first ever truly serious exorcism ritual dedicated to the Satanic path, that is intended to expel an unwanted spirit from an individual person.

There has been three Exorcism rituals created in Satanism, the first was a prayer by Diane Vera, which has been retooled and utilized in this ritual. The second was a full ritual used by the Church of the Four Crowned Princes in Oklahoma as a public show and media stunt. Both of these rites have been focused on blaspheming the Christian god, and are not interested in ousting any real spirits. They are in short, psychodramas intended for a person's mental state alone.

The third is presented here. A compiled collection of prayers, tools, and ritual to be used to effectively remove a hostile spirit from a possessed person.
This exorcism may be performed anywhere, but it is most effectively done in a proper ritual chamber, with the aid of a full Coven or Groto. To perform the ritual certain unique items must be acquired or crafted and blessed on the beforehand.

1. The first and perhaps most important item is what is called "The Devil's Toy box", or "Spirit Cage". This is a simple black box lined with mirrors, and inscribed with runes and sigils to trap and hold a spirit prisoner. There is a curse that is inscribed in the Theban alphabet and spoken in Latin.
2. The second item is a Satanic Rosary. DO NOT USE AN INVERTED CRUSSAFIX! Medallions to use are Sigil of Baphomet, inverted pentacle, Lucifer's cup, Sigwolo pentagram (LaVey's Pentagram), or the sulphur cross (Sigil of brimstone). This item is touch to the possessed's head and chest areas.
3. The third item is blessed water. This is kept in a vial or flask. Blessed water is used to provoke and wound the invading spirit in the exact same way Christians

use holy water. It is one item used to help identify the true nature of the spirit.

ᛉᛏᚺᛃᛦᛘᚢᛉ ᛚᚺᛉᚢ ᚢᚺ ᛉᛈᛏᛚᚱᛉᛉ ᛦ ᛉᛏᚺᛏᛉᛦᛘ
ᛘᛏᛤᛉᛏᛘᛉᚢᛉᛘ ᚢᚺ ᛘᛃᛦᛉᛃᛘᚢᛉᚢᛘ ᛦ ᛉᚢᛘᛦᛉᛉ
ᚢᛉᛈᛏᛘᚢᛘ ᛦ ᛣᚢᛘᛉᚢᛘ ᛘᛏᛉᛉᚢᛉᛦᛦᛉ ᛦ ᛉᛏᛘ ᚺᛘᛉᚢᚺᚺ
ᛉᛉᚢᛏᛉ ᛘᚢᛘᛃᛉᛉᚢᛘᚺ ᛉᛤᚢᛤᛏᛘᚢ ᛉᛉ ᛤᛦᛃᛏᚢᛦ ᛉᛏᛉᚢᛦ ᛉᛉ
ᛤᚢᚺᛤᚱᛉ ᛉᛉ ᛤᛦᛃᛉᛉ ᛦᛘ ᛘᛉᚺᛉ ᛉᛏᛉᛉᛈᛉ ᛦ ᛉᛏᚺᛦᛘᚢᛦ ᛦᛉᛉ
ᛉᛉᛤᛏᛘᚢᛘᛉᚢ ᛉᛉᛉᚢᛉ ᛦ ᛉᚢᛘᛦ ᛤᚢᚢᛉ ᛉᛉᛉᛈᛏᛘ ᛦ

Figure 1 Sigils and Theban script of Devil's Toy Box.

Perhaps more important than tools are people. The exorcist should never work alone, contrary to many movies. The possessed person needs to feel safe. Besides the priest there should be friends and family present to help provide support and assist in any way necessary. Aside from the

123

priest there should be two other critical individuals. A videographer, to record the event. And a trained medical practitioner, to assess and monitor the possessed physical status, and safe guard their health.

In an ideal situation, the exorcism should be performed with the additional aid of a full coven. However, this is seldom the case, so the exorcist must be able to work with outsiders in any sort of situation. Often times he may be forced to deal directly with non-Satanic family and friends. To this end, the exorcist must be cordial to all present and should be capable of explaining the process to others in such a way as to allay their fears and trepidations. This is critical. Unless the exorcist can guarantee the full cooperation of all present, and that they will heed his every command, he cannot perform the exorcism, nor should he.

To this end the only person who should be able to supersede the priests authority once the exorcism has begun is the medical practitioner. And only in the event of critical danger to the possessed or others present. All present must differ to the priest or the medical practitioner at all times for all things, or be ejected from the ritual with no further warning.

As a final little tid-bit. Unlike most rituals, the exorcism has no sword or athame used in it. This is for the safety of all present. There has been accounts of objects taking to the air during exorcisms of the past, and a bladed weapon would not be a good thing to end up having to dodge as one is trying to focus.

Ensure all objects are secure, and that the possessed is secured with appropriate bindings and contained in a salt circle. And it is with that, I present the Rite of Exorcizamus Satanas, the Satanic Exorcism.

The Exorcism

PURIFICATION OF THE AIR
Ring bell 9 times, directing tolling to the four cardinal
compass points while turning counter-clockwise.

INVOCATION TO SATAN
Celebrant faces the Sigil of the Baphomet with arms spread
gently with palms open. The basic invocation is intoned by
Celebrant.

In nomine Dei nostri Satanas Luciferi excelsi!

In the name of Satan, the Ruler of the earth, the King of the
world, I command the forces of Darkness to bestow their
Infernal power upon me!
Open wide the gates of Hell and come forth from the abyss
to greet me as your brother (sister) and friend!
Grant me the indulgences of which I speak! I have taken
thy name as a part of myself! I live as the beasts of the
field, rejoicing in the fleshly life! I favor the just and curse
the rotten! By all the Gods of the Pit, I command that these
things of which I speak shall come to pass!
Come forth and answer to your names by manifesting my
desires!

OH HEAR THE NAMES!

Congregation repeats each name after Celebrant.

THE INFERNAL NAMES

Abaddon	Baalberith	Cimeries
Euronymous	Mammon	Cthulhu
O-ama	Sedit	Anton LaVey
Adramelech	Balaam	Coyote
Fenriz	Mania	Milcom
Pan	Sekhmet	Thamuz
Ahpuch	Baphomet	Dagon
Gorgo	Mantus	Moloch
Pluto	Set	Thoth
Ahriman	Bast	Damballa
Haborym	Marduk	Mormo
Proserpine	Shaitan	Tunrida
Amon	Beelzebub	Demogorgon
Hecate	Mastema	Naamah
Pwcca	Shamad	Typhon
Apollyn	Behemoth	Diabolus
Ishtar	Melek Taus	Nergal
Rimmon	Shiva	Yaotzin
Asmodeus	Beherit	Vlad Dracula
Kali	Mephistopheles	Nihasa
Sabazios	Yog-Sothoth	Yen-lo-Wang
Astaroth	Supay	Emma-O
Lilith	Bilé	Nija
Sammael	Metztli	O-Yama
Azazel	T'an-mo	Shub-Nigguath
Loki	Chemosh	
Samnu	Mictian	
Nyarlathotep	Tchort	

Celebrant: "Arise oh Gods of the Abyss and manifest thy presence through thy blessing."

IV. SUMMONING THE PRINCES OF HELL

Celebrant makes the sign of the horns and points towards the domain of the Prince to be called.

Celebrant: "From the south I summon thee almighty Satan. Come forth oh Lord of the Inferno, I bid thee welcome!"

"From the east I summon thee great Lucifer. Come forth oh Bearer of Light, I bid thee welcome!"

"From the north I summon thee fearsome Belial. Come forth oh King of the Earth, I bid thee welcome!"

"From the west I summon thee dread Leviathan. Come forth oh Dragon of the Abyss, I bid thee welcome!"

"Shemhamforash!"

Congregation. (responds): "Shemhamforash!"

Celebrant: "Hail Satan!"

Congregation. (responds): "Hail Satan!"

V. BENEDICTION

Celebrant: "For though art a mighty Lord, oh Satan, and from thee arises all potency, justice, and dominion. Let our visions become reality and our creations endure, for we are your kindred, demon brethren, and scions of carnal joy." "Satan, give to us thy blessing."

"Lucifer, grant to us thy favor."

"Belial, confer upon us thy benisons."

"Leviathan, bestow to us thy treasures."

COMPASION

Celebrant: W ITH the anger of anguish and the wrath of the stifled, I pour forth my voices, wrapped in rolling thunder that you may hear!
Oh great lurkers in the darkness, oh guardians of the way, oh minions of the might of Thoth! Move and appear!
Present yourselves to us in your benign power, in behalf of one who believes and is stricken with torment.
Isolate him/her in the bulwark of your protection, for he/she is undeserving of anguish and desires it not.
Let that which bears against him/her be rendered powerless and devoid of substance.
Succor him/her through fire and water, earth and air, to regain what he/she has lost.
Strengthen with fire the marrow of our friend and companion, our comrade of the Left-and Path.
Through the power of Satan let the earth and its pleasures re-enter his/her being.
Allow his/her vital salts to flow unhampered, that he/she may savor the carnal nectars of his/her future desires.
Strike dumb his/her adversary, formed or formless, that he/she may emerge joyful and strong from that which afflicts him her.
Allow no misfortune to allay his/her path, for he she is of us, and therefore to be cherished.
Restore him/her to power, to joy, to unending dominion over the reverses that have beset him/her.

Build around and within him /her, the exultant radiance that will herald his/her emergence from the stagnant morass which engulfs him/her.

This we command, in the name of Satan, whose mercies flourish and whose sustenance will prevail!

As Satan reigns so shall his/her own whose name is as this sound: (name) is the vessel whose flesh is as the earth; life everlasting, world without end! Shemhamforash! Hail Satan!

Gong is struck following congregants' response to "Shemhamforash!" and "Hail Satan!"

Sixteenth Key Enochian Intonement
EE-luh-suh • VEEV mah-luh-pee-REE-jzhee ZAH-luh-mahn • DAY DOH-nahss-doh-gah-MAH-tahss-tohss DAHSS • ah-kuh-ROH-ohd-zee BUH-vuh-zuhd, • buh-lee-OH-rahks bah-LEET; • DAHSS • EEN-SSEE kah-OHSSK • LUH-zuh-dahn puh-vuh-ruh-JZHAYL; • mee-KAH-luh-zoh kuh-HEES • SAY-TAN • OHD FAH-fayn! zah-KAH-ray • KAH • OHD ZAH-muh-rahn! • OH-doh KEE-kuh-lay • KAH-ah! ZOR-ruh-jzhay! • ZEE-ruh NOH-koh! • hoh-AH-tuh-huh SAY-TAN • BUH-vuh-fuhd LOH-nuh-suh • LOH-nuh-doh bah-BAH-jzhay

Eighteenth Key Enochian Intonement
EE-luh-suh • mee-kah-OH-luhts OH-luh-PEE-ruh-tuh • OHD MAH-luh-puh-ruh-jzhuh • buh-lee-OHR-ay DAHSS • OH-doh • BUH-vuh-zuhd DAY • SAY-TAN • oh-voh-AH-ruh-suh kah-OHS-suh-goh, • kah-SAH-ruh-muhjzh mee-kah-OH-luhts • KEE-kuh-lays voh-OH-ahn • buh-REE-nuh-tuhs kah-fah-FAHM • DAHSS • EE VUH-MUHD • AH • KUH LOH-nuh-doh • vuh-GAY-ahr DAY • MAHTS • OHD mah-OH-fuh-fahss. BOH-luhp KOH-moh • buh-lee-

OH-ruh-tuh PAH-muh-buh-tuh. zah-KAH-ray • KAH •
OHD ZAH-muh-rahn! • OH-doh KEE-kuh-lay • KAH-ah!
ZOR-ruh-jzhay! • ZEE-ruh NOH-koh! • hoh-AH-tuh-huh
SAY-TAN • BUH-vuh-fuhd LOH-nuh-suh • LOH-nuh-doh
bah-BAH-jzhay

Prayers of Exorcism

In the name of Azazel most holy, great Satan, and almighty
Lucifer!
I hereby command that the spirit of evil and hate, depart
from this mind, this body, and this soul at once!
Be gone thou foul spirit of deception, hypocrisy and
ignorance!
By the midnight brilliance of Lucifer, the Lord, I recognize
thee for the pitiful vampire thou art, and I invoke the power
of the Adversary to bind thee, and keep thee from
infringing upon the freedom of the soul!
Bow before me, encramped spook!
Thou art naught but a vengeful ghost to the ever jubilant
Gods of this World!
In the name of Azazel, we reject thee!
In the name of Satan, we reject thee!
In the name of Lucifer, we reject thee!
Depart, foul spirit! Depart from this vessel's life and from
his/her soul!
Thou cannot refuse my command, for it is no less than a
servant and child of the Prince of Darkness Himself, whom
commands you!
Here me now specter of evil!
I command thee by the names and seals of the crowned
lords of the pit, reveal now thy name!

Continue this portion until spirit reveals its name. Once it has spoken its name, you may proceed to the curse section or complete this section without further asking for the spirits name. Should it refuse, utilize the following enochian calls and or latin exorcism prayer. After each call or prayer demand its name again. Continue this process until the name is given.

The First Key Enochian Intonment
OHL • ZOH-nuhf • voh-ruh-SAH-jzhuh GO-ho • SAY-TAN • LOH-nuh-suh • KAH-luhtz OHD • VOH-ruhss • kah-OHS-suh-goh; ZOH-buh-rah • ZOHL • ROH-ruh EE • TAH • NAHTS-puh-suh OHD • guh-RAH-ah • TAH MAH-luh-puh-ruh-jzhuh: • DAHSS • HOH-luh-kah KAH-AH • noh-tuh-HOH-ah • ZEE-muhts • OHD KOH-muh-mah • TAH • NOH-buh-loh zee-AYN • OHD • LOO-SEEF-tee-uhn OH-boh-lay • AH DOH-nahss-doh-gah-MAH-tahss-tohss OH • oh-hoh-RAY-lah • TAH-bah • OHL NOH-ray • OHD • PAH-suh-buhs • OHL zoh-nuh-RAY-nuh-suhjzh vah-OH-ahn • OHD toh-OH-aht • NOH-noo-KAH-fay guh-MEE-kah-luh-ZOH-mah • PEE-lah FAH-ruh-zuhm • zuh-nuh-ruh-JZHAH • OHD ZOO-ruh-jzhahs • AH-duh-nah • OHD GOH-noh • DAY • SAY-TAN • DAHS • HOHM OHD • TOH • ZOH-bah • kuh-ROH-ohd-zee EE-pahm • OOL • VUH-LUHS • ee-PAH-meess DAHSS • loh-HOH-loh • Vayp noh-tuh-HOH-ah • poh-AH-mahl • OHD BOH-guh-pah • ah-AH-ee • TAH • PEE-ahp pee-AH-mohl OHD • vah-OH-ahn • zah-KAH-ray • KAH OHD • ZAH-muh-rahn! • OH-doh KEE-kuh-lay • KAH-ah! • ZOH-ruh-jzhay! ZEE-ruh • NOH-koh! • hoh-AH-tuh-huh SAY-TAN • BUH-vuh-fuhd • LOH-nuh-suh LOH-nuh-doh • bah-BAH-jzhay

Latin prayer verse 1

Exorcizamus te, omnis spiritus impetum odio et potestas, omnis incursio adversarius noster invehitur omnis exercitus omnis congregatio et secta componantur. Ergo draco maledicte spirituum adjuramus te. Cessa decipere humanas creaturas, et dabo tibi venenum perditionem.

I command you spirit! Reveal to me your name! In the name of Satan! Lucifer! And all things formed and formless! I compel you to speak your name!

The Third Key Enochian Intonement
MEE-kuh-mah! • GOH-ho • SAY-TAN, ZEE-ruh • koh-muh-SAY-luh • AH zee-AYN • BEE-ah • OHSS • LOH-nuh-doh. AIM kuh-HEES • oh-tuh-HEEL JZHEE-JZHEE-pah • vuh-nuh-duh—LUH kuh-HEES • TAH • puh-VEEM • KUH MOH-suh-puh-lay • tay-LOH-kuh kuh-VEE-EEN • toh-luh-TOH-ruhjzh kah-OHS-suh-gah • kuh-HEESSEE OHD • kuh-HEESS • GAY • EM • OH-zee-ayn, DAHSS • TAH buh-ruh-guh-DOH • OHD • TOH-ruht-sool! ah-kuh-ROH-ohd-zee • ay-OHLL bah-luh-ZAH-ruhjzh, • OHD • ah-AH-lah OHSS • tuh-HEE-luhn • NAY-tah-ahb, duh-luh-vuh-JZHAH • voh-muh-SAH-ruhjzh LOH-nuh-sah • kah-puh-mee-AH-lee • VOH-ruhss • AIM • HOH-meel KOH-kuh-suhb, • FAH-fayn, • ee-ZEE-zohp • OHD • mee-ee-NOH-ahjzh DAY • guh-NAY-tah-ahb, • VAH-vuhn • LOH-nuh-suh: pah-nuh-PEE-ruh mah-luh-pee-REE-jzhee • PEE-lahd kah-OHSSK. • NOH-ahn • vuh-NAH-lah BAH-luh-tuh • OHD • voh-OH-ahn. • AH SAY-TAN'S • doh-OH-ay-een, • TOH-ruht-soo! ZAH-mah-rahn! • MEE-kuh-mah! ee-AY-huh-vuh-zohz • Kah-KAH-kohm! doh-OH-ay-een • NO-ahr • mee-kah-OH-luhts ah-AH-ee • OHM! • kuh-SAH-ruh-muhjzh goh-HEE-yah: • ZAH-kahr! • TOH-ruht-soo! ee-

132

muh-VAH-mahr • puh-vuh-GOH! puh-vuh-GOH • puh-LAH-puh-lee KEE-kuh-lays • KAH-AHN!

Latin prayer verse 2

Abiero, Spiritus Domini rapuit et fallaciae, hostis humanae vitae.
Humiliare sub potenti manu inferni Orcus. Contremisce et effuge! Invocato a nobis sancto et terribili sanctoque quem inferi tremunt atque gaudere.

Again I ask your name spirit! You are compelled by me and the Devine!

The Eighth Key Enochian Intonement
BAH-zuhm, • OH, • EE • TAH • AH DOO-waht, • OH-luhn • NAHZTS ah-VAH-buh, • kuh-SAH-ruh-muhjzh vuh-RAHN • kuh-HEES • vuh-GAYJZH DAHSS • ah-buh-RAH-muhjzh BAH-luh-teem • GO-ho • SAY-TAN; ZOH-bah • ah-PEE-lah • OHD BOH-guh-pah • GOH-hud. kuh-HEE-ruh-lahn! • AH • BUH-vuh-zuhd DAY • VOH-veem • AH-ruh • EE HOH-muh-toh • OHD • GOH-hud! EE-ruh-jzheel • kuh-HEES • DAHSS pah-AH-ohx • EE • BUH-vuh-zuhd • DAY kah-OHS-suh-goh • DAHSS • kuh-HEES OHD • EEP • vuh-RAHN • tay-LOH-ah KAH-kuh-ruhjzh • ee-YAHD • guh-NAH-ee LOH-nuh-kuh-hoh • OHD • FAH-fayn guh-NAH-ee • KAH-ruh-bahf? nee-EESS-oh BAH-guh-lay • ah-vah-VAH-goh ee-YOH-ruh! nee-EESS-oh • BAH-guh-lay zee-AH-ee-ohn • OHD • MAH-buh-sah DAY • SAY-TAN • tah-REE-ahn MOH-mahr • OHD • kuh-HEES • REE-pee-ruh poh-EE-luhp. nee-EESS! • ZAH-muh-rahn! KEE-ah-OH-fee • kah-OHS-suh-goh, • OHD Buh-lee-OH-rus • OHD • KOH-ruh-see • TAH kuh-HEES • ah-buh-RAH-meejzh!

Latin prayer verse 3
Insidias ab hoc malo, libera nos, domine satanas. Ut
Ecclesiam tuam secura tibi facias libertate servire, te
rogamus, audi nos. Ut inimicos sanctae Ecclesiae humiliare
Te rogámus, audi nos!

By the powers of Hell, and the Black Flame! Surrender thy
name spirit!

Spirit Cage Curse: The Devils Toy Box
I know thee (names of spirit)! Be gone thou vile spirit, and
leave this world in peace!

In the name of Azazel the Prince, I cast thee OUT!
In the name of Leviathan the Dragon, I cast thee OUT!
In the name of Lilith the Mother, I cast thee OUT!
In the name of Lucifer the Light Bringer, I cast thee OUT!
In the name of Satan the Adversary and King, I cast thee
OUT!

For thou art cursed for all time (name of spirit)!

Priest presents the box open before possessed and recites
the curse. When done the lid is closed and sealed, then
replaced on the alter.
Tenebris quasi in speculo. Tenetur reflectitur in
obumbratio. Exutus imperio. Gratia destitutum. Per nomina
etiam diabolica Luciferi et cubavit Lamia es vincula se
habet ad omne tempus. Penuria vos maledicti estis. Sic fiat
semper.

RITE OF THE CHALICE

Celebrant: "As our prayers ascends to thee, Infernal Lord, so shall your blessings descend upon us."

Bless chalice with the mudras of flames.

Celebrant: "Lord Satan, Imperator of Fire, Hell and Earth are filled with your glory. Hosanna in profundis!"

Celebrant elevates chalice.

Celebrant: "Behold the chalice of ecstasy filled with the elixir of life. As kindred to the undefiled beasts, I drink and celebrate the Black Flame within."

Celebrant drinks and says: "Satan, thy strength is mine!"

Celebrant turns to offer chalice to the previously possessed with these words:

Celebrant: "Drink and honor thy true nature."

They drink and reply:

Participant: "The Black Flame burns within me. Satan, thy strength is mine!"

Celebrant faces altar and elevates chalice a final time.

Celebrant: "Hail Satan!"

Congregation. (responds): "Hail Satan!"

Celebrant replaces the chalice on altar.

Baptism

At this point it is wise to perform a new baptism on the possessed, to help prevent re-infestation by any spirits. This also reaffirms the possessed personal faith and beliefs. The exorcist may use this modified LaVeyan baptism or create one of his own suitable for this instance. If restrained the possessed is freed of their bonds. This section can be ignored if desired and the ritual closed, but it is recommended that it is kept in. For children use the childs baptism found in the satanic rituals.

PRIEST:

In the majestic light of undefiled wisdom, awake and enter into the Arcadian Wood wherein all thy lingering falsehoods shall be as dead bark, stripped from thy trunk: where thy futile hypocrisies, known and unknown, shall no longer envelop thee in mind and body. Thou mayest breathe again, that first breath now as night winds freshen from the far reaches of Belial.

Preist anoints the possessed head with the sacred water in the sign of the inverted pentagram.

PREIST:

I bless the child of nature. With the waters of sacred undefiled wisdom. By the terrible and sacred names if the Kings and Queens of Hell, I give thee new life.

Priest then places amulet around possessed's neck, while saying:

PRIEST:

I place the amulet of Baphomet upon you, and therewith seal thy eternal commitment to Satan, Lord of thy chosen realm, and thy unyielding loyalty to the wondrous order of His creation. Raise thy right hand in the Sign of the Horns and receive this, thine oath: Thou, who have forsworn the divine mindlessness, do proclaim the majesty of thine own being amongst the marvels of the universe. Thou rejecteth oblivion of self, and accepteth the pleasure and pain of unique existence. Thou art returned from death to life, and declareth thy friendship with Lucifer, Lord of Light, who is exalted as Satan. Thou receiveth the Sigil of Baphomet and embraceth the black flame of cherished enlightenment. Thou hath assumed this Infernal commitment of thine own volition, without let or hindrance: this act being done without coercion and of thine own desire and according to thy will.

Priest faces possessed and, with the sign of the horns, describes with it an inverted pentagram. It is traced in the air directly in front of the initiate's chest and the newly consecrated amulet. Priest and initiate face altar and present again the Sign of the Horns.

PRIEST:
Hail, Satan!

POSSESSED: Hail, Satan!

POLLUTIONARY/ Closing the Rite.
Celebrant rings bell as at the beginning. When the sounds have decayed into silence the Celebrant concludes:

Celebrant: "So it is done!"

Celebrant extinguishes remaining illuminating candles or other light sources if this is out of doors, ending the ceremony.

Funeral for Satanic Familiars & Pets

The love of an animal is unconditional. This statement has been proven true time and again. It can be unexpected when one of Nature's creatures wiggles its way into our lives. They bring us friendship, joy, and love.

We stop seeing them as just an animal and welcome them as beloved family members. We often wonder who is smarter. Us for teaching and taking care of them. Or our little friends for getting us to let them freeload from us for nothing more than a tail wag or a purring nuzzle.

As with all living things though, life can be very painful, especially when the time comes to say goodbye. The death of a beloved animal can hurt just as bad as any other beloved family member.

The following ritual is adapted from the Church of Satan funeral ritual and the All Hallows Mass, to help say good bye to our companions when that time comes.

The Ritual Proper
I. PURIFICATION OF THE AIR
Ring bell 9 times, directing tolling to the four cardinal compass points while turning counter-clockwise. The "Hymn to Satan" may be played simultaneously.

II. INVOCATION TO SATAN
Celebrant: "Arise, oh Gods of the abyss, and attend those who celebrate the life of one who was thy kith and kin in animal form.

Open wide the adamantine gates and fly out to greet one who has moved beyond our pack. Take them under your leathered wings and guide to the place of waiting.

Come forth now and answer to your names.

The Infernal Names:

"Anubis, Bastet, Gorgo, Mormo, Tezcatlipoca, Nija, Hecate, Mictian, Pluto, Proserpine, Mania, Yaotzin, Supay, Mantus, Emma-o, Nergal, Yen-lo-Wang"

Congregation repeats each name after Celebrant.

IV. SUMMONING THE PRINCES OF HELL

Celebrant takes sword and points towards the domain of the Prince to be called.

Celebrant: The south is a land of sunlight and fire, and your flames guide us through the cycles of life. Satan Lord of fire, we welcome you, knowing you will transform us in death.

The east is a land of new beginnings, the place where breath begins.
Lucifer Lord of the air, we call upon you, knowing you will be with us as we depart life.

The north is a place of cold, and the earth is silent and dark. Belial Lord of the earth, we welcome you, knowing you will envelope us in death.

The west is a place of underground rivers, and the sea is a never-ending, rolling tide. Leviathan Lord of the waters, we welcome you, knowing you will carry us through the ebbs and flows of our lives.

"Shemhamforash!"

Congreg. (responds): "Shemhamforash!"

Celebrant: "Hail Satan!"

Congreg. (responds): "Hail Satan!"

Gong is struck.

Celebrant replaces sword on altar.

V. BENEDICTION

"Satan, give to us thy blessing.

Lucifer, grant to us thy favor.

Belial, confer upon us thy benisons.

Leviathan, bestow to us thy treasures."

VIII. THE FUNERARY INVOCATION

Celebrant: "Glory to thee, almighty Satan, highest and ineffable King of Hell; and on Earth, joy to the followers of the Left-Hand Path. Oh potent Prince of Darkness, thou grandest us vital existence and undefiled wisdom."

"Ever living Lord of the Pit, who has willed that all the pleasures of the flesh shall be made manifest, grant to thy disciples' remembrance of [Togar], one of the children of the night who reveled in thy nature, who was truly born to be among thy chosen. Hail [Togar]!"

Congreg. (responds): "Hail [Togar]!"

Celebrant: "Tonight we mourn the loss of a friend and animal [brother/sister], a fellow God. Without you, our worlds are lessened indeed."

"We celebrate [Togar] and all [his/her] extraordinary being. [He/She] embraced us as their packmates because [he/she] chose to be loving of us despite the face of the vastness of our different natures.
[He/She] was a wonderous friend to us. *(If a dog, [He/She] was a ruthless protector to any who stood against [his/her] pack.)* Our world is ever in need of outstanding individuals like [Togar]. Shemhamforash!"

Congreg. (responds): "Shemhamforash!"

Celebrant: "Hail Satan!"

Congreg. (responds): "Hail Satan!"

Gong is struck.

IX. THE MEMORIAL

Celebrant: "Come forth, and bid our friend [Togar] you farewell."

The Celebrant has thus invited the mourners to approach him at the Altar Shrine. One at a time, those who wish to may come up, each facing the congregation, and speak about their memories and love and respect for the deceased. This part of the rite may include spoken testimonials, the reading of passages from books which were important to the deceased, the playing of music of significance (recorded or performed live), the reading of poetry, telling of favored jokes, showing of video, and so on. Any presentation, which brings the memories of the deceased most vividly to mind, is acceptable. The intent is to bring an emotional catharsis wherein weeping is expected, as the loss is felt most deeply. But also, finally, we mean to incite joy, as each congregant treasures the memories of the person whose life has ended, as well as the marvelous things produced during that life, and share this with the other mourners.

X. PASSING OF THE BLACK FLAME

When all of the memorials have been presented, the Celebrant invites all the mourners to approach the Shrine Altar with these words:

Celebrant: "Unholy brethren, these many deeds wrought by [Togar] remain with us. Come forward and accept this token of [Togar]'s gifts to you."
As they do, he hands each of them a black candle, which They then proceed to light at the Black Flame candle (Celebrant or an assistant may help them).
Appropriate music may be played during this process.
After receiving the candle, each mourner quietly says "Hail [Togar]!"

The mourners return to their places and stand, holding the burning candles, meditating on the thought that this flame symbolizes the vitality that was shared with them by the deceased.

After the final mourner has returned to his place the Celebrant continues:
"Dear [Togar], long shall you live in the hearts of those you inspired."

"You enjoyed life to the fullest—fanning the fires about you, igniting in those fortunate enough to be near a part of your passion for the pleasures of this world."

"As you are borne out upon the Ebon river, to be embraced by Darkness Eternal, you continue to touch us with your magic."

"We shall always cherish the gifts you have bestowed upon us, as they bring us deep satisfaction, and spur us on to our own achievements."

"We salute thee, [Togar], comrade of the Left-Hand Path, one who is truly numbered among Hell's chosen, who moved with elegance and might within the Devil's fane." Celebrant now moves to the Black Flame Candle:

"Good night, sweet [Prince]."

Celebrant extinguishes the candle.

"Your flame has been spent, yet it burns ever brightly within our hearts."

Congreg: "Good night, [Togar]."

Mourners now extinguish their candles. They may keep these to use for future meditations upon the gifts from the deceased.

TRANSITIONAL:

A. If there is to be a burial, the rite is not closed but will end at the gravesite when the mourners re-assemble. It would be preferable for this to take place at night, or twilight.

Celebrant: "Kinsmen of [Togar Szandor LaVey], we go now to gather at the appointed place."

The mourners now leave the chamber quietly and go to the place of burial. If it is necessary to drive, a traditional funerary procession of vehicles may now take place. It is preferable for the vehicles to be white in color. When all have assembled at the graveside, the rite may continue with the closing.

B. If the body has been cremated and the remains are kept, then the closing rite follows immediately.

C. If the remains are to be scattered now, the rite is not closed but is concluded when the mourners have assembled at the spot for the scattering. The Celebrant uses the same words of invitation to re-assemble as above in "A."
If the scattering will take place at an indeterminate later time, the closing rite is follows, and those present at the scattering may repeat the closing rite, or other appropriate words, at that time.

XI. THE CLOSING RITE

Celebrant: "Attend, dear fellows. We give a sign of our allegiance to the Powers of Darkness with these words received from an unknown hand."

The Eleventh Enochian Key is read by the Celebrant.

"I bid thee rise and give the Sign of the Horns.
(If standing, 'I bid thee give the Sign of the Horns.')"

Congregation responds as bidden with the salute, given with the left hand.

Celebrant: "The gates of Hell have opened and the Lords of the Netherworld have drawn near! [Togar] reveled in this world of worlds, and as a member of our pack [he/she] shall live in the hearts and memories of those who adored [him/her] throughout [his/her] lifetime, as long as the breath of life shall sustain them."

The Rainbow Bridge
For Other Familiars and Pets
Just this side of the Stix, along its murky banks is a place called Rainbow Bridge. It's not quite Heaven, and not quite Hell. It's not grim or brooding, but a place of peace and rest. A place without judgement.

When an animal dies that has been especially close to someone here, that pet goes to Rainbow Bridge. There are meadows and hills for all of our special friends so they can run and play together. There is plenty of food, water and sunshine, and our friends are warm and comfortable.

All the animals who had been ill and old are restored to health and vigor. Those who were hurt or maimed are made whole and strong again, just as we remember them in our dreams of days and times gone by. The animals are happy and content, except for one small thing; they each miss someone very special to them, who had to be left behind. They all run and play together, but the day comes when one, or possibly a group of them, suddenly stops and looks into the distance. Their bright eyes are intent, and eager bodies quiver.

Suddenly they begin to run from the rest of animals, flying over the green grass. Their legs, wings, fins, flippers, or whatever carrying them faster and faster.

You have been spotted, and when you and your special friend/s finally meet, you cling together in joyous reunion, never to be parted again. The happy kisses rain upon your face; your hands again caress the beloved head, feathers, or scales and you look once more into the trusting eyes of your

pet, so long gone from your life but never absent from your heart.
Then you cross Rainbow Bridge together....

"By all the powers of Satan let [Togar] await us at the Rainbow Bridge forever and ever; until the day comes we meet again, and may [his/her] final place of rest lie all the way to Hell. To this we say these final words"

Continue onward to the appropriate sections for you pets species or write a custom entry.

For a Cat
Short Prayer to Say Goodbye
You have crossed over now,
into the spirit realm.
May you walk with Bast,
and I will see you again someday.

A Prayer to Return to the Earth
Mother Earth, we return to you
the body of one of your children.
Her spirit will return to her ancestors,
and she will continue to live in our memories.
We are thankful that we were able
to share our lives with her,
and give her to your loving arms.

Prayer to Bast and Sekhmet
Bast, Sekhmet, we give you back your child.
Noble, regal, honorable cat.
Watch over her, and guide her on her way
to the spirit world.

May she be blessed in your names,
and hunt ever after beside you.

For a Dog
Short Prayer to Say Farewell
Faithful friend, loyal companion,
we say farewell to you now.
You have kept us warm at night,
protected our home
and offered us unconditional love.
For this we are thankful,
and we will remember you forever.

Prayer to Honor the Wild Spirit
In days gone by, the dog ran wild, untamed and free.
Although man may have tamed your bodies,
we have never tamed your spirit.
You are free now.
Go and run with your pack,
with your wild ancestors, racing by the midnight moon.
Go and hunt for your prey,
taking what is your birthright.
Join the wolf, the jackal, the wild dogs,
and run with your kin on the wild hunt.
Run, and guide your spirit home.

Prayer to the Gods of the Pack
Hail to you, Anubis, and may you protect this dog
as he runs to the afterlife.
Hail to you, Kerberos, guardian of the gates,
watcher of the land beyond,
may you welcome this dog to the next place.
Hail to you, Wepwawet, opener of the roads,
may you take this dog to stand beside you,
brave and loyal in life and death.
Hail to you, loyal pet, and may you be blessed
as you run into the sunset to the west,

chasing the stars into the night,
one final time.

Celebrant (CONGREG. repeats):
"Shemhamforash!"
"Hail Satan!"
"Hail [Togar]!"
"Hail [Togar]!"
"Hail [Togar]!"

Gong, if present, is struck following congregant's repetition of "Hail Satan!" and "Hail [Togar]!"

XII. POLLUTIONARY
Celebrant rings bell as at the beginning, while "Hymn to Satan" or music dear to the deceased is played. When the sounds have decayed into silence the Celebrant concludes:

Celebrant: "So it is done!"

Celebrant extinguishes remaining illuminating candles (or other light sources if this is out of doors), and all experience the darkness for a moment. Conventional illumination is then restored, ending the ceremony.

XIII. REPASS
It is then traditional for the mourners to gather for food and drink, as this signifies the continuance of vital existence.

The Consecrations of a Black House

The strange dreams in which I had encountered what I believe to be the genuine spirit of Anton Szandor LaVey, brought with them many revelations. These revelations have influenced me to be very customized and diverse with each individual ritual I perform choosing not to stick to cookie cutter molds.

Often times in the various encounters I've had with the founder of our religion, it seldom goes beyond mild banter, and is very uneventful, though often rather humorous. We may discuss people we know or knew, and comment on our feelings. Sometimes the commentary is not always flattering.

It was in one of my more recent encounters that I had a discussion with him about how to sanctify a Black House properly. I have already gone over some of the basic details of this conversation at length in a previous chapter. Here we will discuss my personal take away from the conversation and provide an in depth formula to the performance of said rituals.

Before we do that though we must answer a few vital questions first.
- Question. What is a Black House?
- Answer. A Black House is a privately owned house that is the residence and place of religious practice, of a Satanic Priest.
- Question. Why is it called a "Black House"?
- Answer. While not always the case these houses are often painted black to reflect their nature and as a salute to the original Black House owned and established by Anton LaVey. This famous structure has since been destroyed by the city of San Francisco.
- Question. How many Black Houses exist?
- Answer. Several structures bare the moniker of "Black House" most are only in the loosest of terms, while a few are in the more literal sense of the term. Currently to the best of my personal knowledge only two homes hold this title in the most literal sense. Magus Peter Gilmores residence in Poughkeepsie NY. And my own residence, Firethorn Manor.
- Question. Have all Black houses been fully sanctified?
- Answer. No. If I am to understand my dreams correctly, the three steps to a full consecration of a Black House have only been accomplished once at the time of writing this. And that was by LaVey himself.

- Question. Why has no one else performed these three rites?
- Answer. No one outside a small group of people knew about them and only an even smaller group had any details on their performance. This group does not include the current heads of the Church of Satan to the best of my knowledge.
- Question. If the heads of the Church don't know about it then, how do you? And what proof do you have to support your claims?
- Answer. The knowledge was relayed to me by what I believe to be the actual spirit of Anton LaVey in a dream. I have no proof backing my claims save for the description of a room that to the best of my knowledge was never seen by anyone but LaVey's closest friends and family members. And that is of what I believe to be his study. A room at the top of his house the ceiling slanted in. The walls lined with hundreds possibly thousands of books. There are piles of books everywhere, and a few chairs to sit in. At the front of this room by a window is a very cluttered desk with his type-writer on it.
- Question. Why is it important to have a Black House?
- Answer. Black Houses are vital sources of power. Not any house can be a Black House. And that is what makes them so special when a one is established with full sanctification in place. Due to the restrictive nature of creating one, only certain Satanist can even begin to establish a Black House. What is more is if my dreams are correct only one has ever existed in a completed state.

The First Ritual
A Simple House Blessing

Start by gathering the ingredients found in the Satanic Scriptures for a consecration of an item. The principle is the same only on a large scale. The ritual begins in what will become the Formal Ritual Chamber. It will also be closed in this same room.

The ritual is opened in the basic method found in the Satanic Bible or a custom opening may be performed.

Create the sacred water with salts and have incense or white sage ready. White sage is preferred as it is known for cleansing homes of unwanted energy. Use a small vial or aspergillum to hold and sprinkle the sacred water.

Always start with the water from the center of the room anointing each wall thrice. Repeating at each wall the following.

In nomine Dei nostril Satanas Luciferi excelsi!
In the name of Satan!
Who is Lucifer!
And by all the host of Hell!
Bless this home Oh Lords of the inferno,
and grant its residence your protection from all ills.

Next walk the perimeter of the room stopping at each corner with the burning sage and thrice sage the corner repeating the same blessing as before.

Do this in every room of the house. Hallways, kitchens, bathrooms, attics and basements, also count as rooms, and must be blessed is as efficient a manner as possible.

When finished return to the starting room and close the ritual out in the prober manner ending with the words, "So it is done!"

The Second Ritual
Consecration of the Black Altar

The second Ritual described by LaVey was the consecration of the altar. This ritual is a bit different in that it is an outright sex ritual. Truth is it doesn't even really need to be done in a ritualistic fashion. Getting down to the bare bones of it, you basically have sex with a person who is not your partner or spouse, and definitely of the opposite biological gender on the altar itself. The altar is then consecrated with the resulting fluids mixed in the womb of the female participant.

Obviously, this is a sexual encounter that does not make room for any sort of condom or protection save birth control. As such the use of a Sacred Prostitute, is certainly warranted.

It is important to note a few things first.

1. Though this is a ritual, it is more important to have fun and enjoyment in the act, rather than

getting any ritualized formalities correct. The true consecration comes from the carnal pleasure, symbolized by the resulting fluids collected from the womb of the female participant.

2.	The partner in this ritual at no time may be a significant other. This does not mean lying to your significant other, rather the opposite. Their blessing in the action should be paramount. They may even choose to witness the event personally. But they may not participate directly.

3.	Both parties must operate within their biological gender from birth. They should be very comfortable with their birth anatomy. Transgenderism will not function here. Its all natural or nothing.

4.	And lastly. It is of utmost and paramount importance, to remember that this is a ritual act of pure carnal pleasure. Both parties involved need to be fully willing, and committed, to the satisfaction of their carnal needs above all else. The actual acts of sex and "depravity" should never be rushed. If these acts carry on all night, then so be it. If only a few moments that is fine too. What is most important is that the gratification of both parties must be constant and continuous until the said fluids are collected and spread upon the altar.

The
Third Ritual
The Black Mass

Perhaps the most famous of the Satanic Rituals, and the final ritual that is critical to the consecration of a Black House, is the legendary Black Mass. This ritual that is a parody of the Catholic Mass, has seen a number of variations over the years, though for the most part its text and workings remain largely the same. These various changes have often been to address the legal nature of the ritual. Past accounts have involved everything from infanticidal "sacrifices", to questionable acts of near or blatant pedophilia.

There is always a level of sexual under or overtones to the ritual itself. With accounts of outright perversions in most of the rituals described. This is to be expected, given the very nature of the ritual.

The ritual given here is a custom re-editing of the traditional rite. Minus of course and human sacrifices or involvement of children of any sort.

It should also be noted that while a Solitary Black Mass similar to the one performed and filmed on Walpurgisnacht 2019, will suffice, it is assumed that a small group is active and able to perform this rite.

This ritual is best performed with a group of five participants. However, with some adjustments made for numbers this ritual can be performed with as few as three or even two people. But for the sake of clarity this ritual is written with five participants in mind. And yes, this version is a bit heavier on the sexual tones.

Timing is another critical point with this ritual that cannot be ignored. While the traditional time of day to perform such rituals is in the evening, the time of day is of less importance than the day itself. Such a final ritual to create a Black House should always be done either on Walpurgisnacht or some other important Sabbaths or Esbats.

Lucifer LeGivorden

Alexandrue Lucifer Ravensloft LeGivorden, is an active Satanist and ordained Priest into the Priesthood of Hell. He is an expert in the occult with more than two and a half decades of experience in numerous occult and religious fields. He has brought his talents to bear to aid law enforcement, and provide a deeper understanding to the occult world for the layman. He is also one of the few Satanists to be capable of performing Exorcism, and has done so multiple times.

As a child LeGivorden traveled across the globe twice before he was two, and lived in the United Arab Emirates until he was four. After returning to the States, he would accompany his adopted mother on cross country road trips and fostered a deep love for all things strange and mysterious.

LeGivorden has been a jack of all trades over the course of his life and enjoys a variety of accomplishments. He has been an occultist, author, radio personality, underground wrestler, property manager, martial artist, digital and graphic artist, YouTube personality, and most recently a film actor.

Lucifer LeGivorden currently lives in South Carolina, and hopes to finally set down permanent roots with his fiancé and son, and their menagerie of wonderfully quirky pets.